Divine Complement

Divine Complement

The Spiritual Terrain of Soulmate Relationships

Ariadne Green

Palm Leaf Press

For further information, please contact:

Palm Leaf Press
5095 Napilihau St.
109 B. #300
Lahaina, HI 96761
editor@ariadnegreen.com

Book design by:

Arbor Books, Inc.
19 Spear Road, Suite 202
Ramsey, NJ 07446
www.arborbooks.com

Cover design by Melody Swan
Cover Photo by Carolyn Quan, www.carolynquan.com

Printed in the United States

Divine Complement: The Spiritual Terrain of Soulmate Relationships
Ariadne Green

1. Title 2. Author 3. Non-Fiction/Relationships/Soulmates

Library of Congress Control Number: 2006900319
ISBN: 0-9766862-3-6

This Book is Dedicated to **God My Mother**
For creating us two by two.

Acknowledgements

I am grateful to all the Divine Complements whose stories fill this book. Their true-life experiences of love and friendship touched my heart. I want to thank my editor, Toni Robino, Carolyn Quan for her fine art photography of Magdalene's Rose, Melody Swan for the outstanding cover design, Hamish Douglas Burgess of Maui Celtic Designs and Arbor Books for their assistance with production. Special thanks to Barbara Hanger, Heather Weis, and Ruby Grace for their friendship and encouragement.

Table of Contents

The Story of the Twin Centered Rose

(cover photo)

I bought a beautiful bouquet of long-stem red roses for my best friend, Laura, who was in the hospital last autumn. Cancer and the complications of surgery and chemotherapy had pushed her to the threshold of "near-death experience" weeks before. Her recovery was a true miracle—the result of prayer and healing hands.

She asked me to take the roses home with me on the day she was being transferred to a rehab center, where she was to continue her already-lengthy recovery and rehabilitation. As I often do, I asked the Divine Feminine, Mary Magdalene, to bless the roses as I laid them on my altar. They continued to blossom there alongside my pictures of Mary and Jesus for nearly a week.

My dear friend Carolyn Quan, a photographer, was at my home for a dream group on the same evening that I had brought the roses home. I was naturally excited to show her and the other members of my group the splendor of the roses on my altar. Carolyn, with her fine eye for detail, noticed the anomaly of twin buds at the center of the rose that stood front and center in the bouquet. We were all amazed at and in awe of this unusual and splendid rose. Carolyn pulled her digital camera out of her purse in excitement. To our dismay, the display on the camera read "low battery." She had an awful time getting the picture to stay on the viewer so she could snap some shots. I prayed again, this time asking Jesus and Mary to bless Carolyn and her camera. The camera suddenly came on and she was able to get three shots before the camera failed.

Carolyn e-mailed me the photo of the rose within a few days and I gazed into its center several times that hour, marveling at its beauty and rarity. The third time I pulled the image up onto the desktop of my computer, my eye was pulled into the center of each bud, where for the first time I noticed two figures, male and female. I gasped in recognition of them.

What the photo reveals is astonishing—two tiny figures, each nestled within the two buds at the center—Jesus, recognized by dark hair and a chin beard, sitting beneath three palm branches (left bud) and Mary Magdalene, recognized by a long head veil, the customary attire seen in biblical images of women of Judea during the time of Christ, (right bud). The outer petals of the left blossom unfold forming an angelic figure with wings facing right at the center of the rose and the outer petals of the right bud reveal yet another figure whose arms embrace Mary.

The imagery within the rose appears to convey a story in which the transfigured angel, Jesus Christ, emerges from beneath palm branches and redirects his pose to stand before his beloved in recognition of the divinity of their union. Mary sits in repose embraced from behind by the arms of what appear to be an emanation of the Holy Spirit.

Does the rose represent a divine apparition, or is it merely anomaly of nature being subjected to the overly imaginative wanderings of an intuitive mind? The picture presents what was captured in one miraculous moment of divine communication through the lens of an ordinary digital camera. The rose photo was not artistically produced or altered except for its color. Only the thumbnail image on the back cover has been artistically enhanced to point out the location of the tiny figures of Jesus and Mary Magdalene.

What does this miracle manifestation and communication from the Divine suggest?

It suggests to me a confirmation that Mary Magdalene and Jesus were twin souls and beloveds, forever bound in beauty, love and devotion, qualities symbolized the rose. As you will discover in the chapter titled *Sacred Bride and Bridegroom*, there is substantial evidence to support that Jesus and Mary were twin souls and married at the time of Jesus' ministry on Earth. In that chapter, we will examine the message in the imagery of the photo at length, and I will elaborate on my interpretation of its meaning as it relates to the premise of the chapter.

I have lovingly named the photo on the cover *Magdalene's Rose*.

Introduction

"The minute I heard my first love story,
I started looking for you,
not knowing how blind that was.
Lovers don't finally meet somewhere.
They're in each other all along."
—Maulana Jelaluddin Rumi

*J*ust about everyone desires a soul mate. Someone to whom we are divinely connected and who promises to fulfill our life like no one else can. We might call them 'beloved', our 'twin soul' or 'soul mate', but the term that most clearly defines this very real spiritual partnership is Divine Complement.

Research demonstrates that most people believe that there is one person in the world who is their perfect match—their Match Made in Heaven. I ran across a survey conducted by About.com at the end of 2003 that overwhelmingly supports the notion. Participants were asked whether they believe in the theory of soul mates, one person in the world who is tailored for them. Seventy-five percent of the 158 respondents answered "yes." Of the 127 women and 30 men who elaborated on why they believe in the concept of soul mates, most said they believe in a divine destiny with someone who complements them perfectly and whom they are meant to learn from and grow with in this life. Most believe God has a hand in the love equation. Of those who had not yet found the perfect match, most were holding out for their soul mate. Even the majority of those who responded "no" to the survey question said that they believe in the soul-mate concept but that they think there is probably more than one person they're suited for in this life, the notion of multiple soul mates. A study done by the Gallup organization in 2001 for the National Marriage Project offers even more convincing statistics. Out of the 1, 003 married and unmarried twenty to twenty-nine year olds surveyed, 98% said that it was important to them to marry their soul mate. Eight-eight percent said, "there is a special person, a soul mate, waiting for you somewhere out there", and 87% were confident that they would find their soul mate when they were ready for marriage.

Our Divine Complement, we might romanticize is our perfect match, offering us the right amount of positive qualities to suit our ideals. Fitting us like the right shoe, they will walk step by step alongside us through life as a perfect complement and companion. Undoubtedly, they will be someone with whom we can be best friends, bare our soul and plan a great future. They will know what we're thinking without our having to say a word, understanding us better than we even understand ourselves. Their heart will be undoubtedly huge and when beating along side our own will create a melodious and harmonious rhythm. We will become enchanted with them, move passionately toward them, and be delivered to the certainty that God exists within our communion. It will undoubtedly be a love match divinely established, heaven sent, and arriving like a miracle of grace when we least expect it.

Beyond fantasies of perfection, instead by definition, our Divine Complement, simply put, is our twin soul. Perfect in our eyes or not, they represent that one person to whom we are most connected soul-to-soul and spirit-to-spirit, and with whom we may or may not be offered the opportunity to bond to in this life. They hold inborn potentials that match and complement our own and hold the key to our spiritual evolution. They are our ultimate complementary spiritual partner.

Pairing up with our Divine Complement may happen at 16 or 60 or not at all. Despite the fact that everyone has a soul mate, not all will make it to the altar for reasons that will be illuminated later in this book.

Most of us want the "happy ever after", the promise of a meaningful and spiritual relationship. It's not likely that we will attach as much meaning to the relationships that come in and go out of our lives and don't come close to fulfilling that promise. Still, a lot of us fall in love over and over again, thinking that we have just found the "Real Thing"—our Divine Complement.

Each time we enter a new relationship we believe it is the first time, the only time, or the last time we will fall in love with someone. Maybe it is or maybe it isn't. Some lucky people meet their Divine Complement early in life. Perhaps they were high school sweethearts who knew from the start they would be sharing a lifetime together. For most, however, the journey to their Divine Complement or soul mate will be a path with many lead-ins, each one of whom is meant to bring us to the emotional maturity to stand alone, as well as along side a complementary equal. Lead-ins often reflect qualities we may admire in the beginning and end up detesting once the romance is over. We co-create with them numerous scenarios of the patterns of inequality that we must outgrow if we are going to succeed at love and equality within relationship. They can lead us to the cliff and push us to the brink of our capacity to love so that we can love ourselves more and prove that we can express love to others. Each offers us a puzzle piece to the larger picture of our destiny and ushers in the fateful lessons that force us to grow. Once our Divine Complement comes through the door we are likely to feel more prepared for the Real Thing.

For me, the preparation for pairing up was a long journey through which I had to learn something about my own maleness reflected in the many complementary partners who came my way. I remember as a child thinking a lot about the male gender, especially because I grew up in a household of all women. It was a unique upbringing sitting at the table with my mother, aunt and grandmother seldom mentioning the "M" word. "Men." By the time I was nine, I was convinced that that there was something to be learned from the opposite sex. They seemed to possess something that I didn't, a bravery and a way of moving through the world as if they owned it. This intrigued me, a very shy little girl who even at that age was introspective.

My first romance novel was Dick and Jane. I read it over and over again, not to practice my reading skills, but out of desire for the kind of friendship and companionship that someone like Dick might offer. Brother and Sister Buzz, two marionette bees who never ventured too far from each other on adventures galore, was my favorite after school television show. I even had two goldfish, Rollie and Pollie, who seemed meant to swim together for life in a fish bowl. Barbie always had to be paired with Ken. They played doctor often, as did the couple that lived in my tin dollhouse, who had two children, one boy and one girl. I played the board game *Life* for hours with my friends but seemed more interested in getting my masculine complement into my pink vehicle than going to college or making it to the Millionaire Mansion.

My real experiences at this age with male complements were two brothers who lived across the street, Larry and Steve. They were as different as night and day. I gravitated toward the younger of the two, Steve, who on occasion chased me around the yard with the garden hose squirting me with the full force of the nozzle. It hurt and I would scream a lot. I put up with his teasing and taunting just for a little male attention all that year. Much later in life, I put up with even more from the men whom I loved and who tested my personal power. I remember one day Steve offered me a dime if I would pull down my swimsuit to show him my "you know what." That was my first experience with human sexuality, the shame of which I couldn't shake, especially when my grandmother greeted me with an evil eye when I returned from playing across the street.

Having had enough of Steve's antics, I was certain that Larry was the one I could be a real friend to. He was shy and getting more than two words out of him was an ordeal. I watched him a lot from across the street attempting to figure out what was bothering him. I am sure it was an urge to heal him with my compassion. I must confess that I still do that with most men who have come my way.

Steve and Larry moved away, when their dad who was a cameraman for the movie industry ended the shooting of "This Earth Is Mine" starring Rock Hudson in the Napa Valley. They had lived with their grandmother and their dad for about a year in that house across the street. I never really asked where their mother was, but it was all over Larry's face that he was sad about it. Steve, well he was just plain angry. I never mentioned my Dad either, because at the time I didn't know where he was. After they moved away, I stayed connected with their grandmother who made me orange tapioca, the same kind she made for them. She mentioned them from time to time and that kept me reminiscing about the good times in their absence.

My neighborhood was over run with boys during those early years, which I now interpret as a good thing for a little girl who had three grown women to dress, bathe and feed her. My home was a real Queendom and I the littlest princess dreaming for a dad to rescue her from the over abundance of maternal interference. But he never came, not when I was 9 or 10 or even 15. Instead, fate presented me with other complementary examples to fill my heart.

There was another Larry who lived up the street who was fat like me and lived with his mom and grandmother also. And still another Larry who lived across the street from fat Larry who was skinny and whose father was also absent from the home. Larry and Larry always played together and just about every day I would venture up the street to hang out with them. I had three Larry's in that year to offer me a complementary example of male energy and intelligence. What are the chances of that? And all from single parent homes. Coincidence or serendipity?

Having spent my adult life exploring the meaning of dreams, interpreting their symbols and archetypal patterns, I know that our waking life also offers us meaning at every turn if we reflect on its mystery and interpret life as a dream. The names of the characters in our lives can hold significant meaning and often express the authentic qualities of the bearer. The name Larry, or Lawrence, is derived from the laurel, meaning crown. By no coincidence Steven means crown also. I had four crowned princes to emulate that year to begin integrating my masculine side.

Symbolically, a crown denotes authority, honor, victory and glory and is associated with the archetypes of the King and Queen, the rulers of the subconscious, who in balance represent masculine and feminine complementary partners. They are the authentic spiritual aspects of the male and female who in their divine state wear a crown of glory, signifying their connection to God.

The serendipity of four crowns as male complements staged a meaningful play in which at an early age I could learn about masculine consciousness. In retrospect, they each held complementary qualities through which I was to learn something about the active male principle that asserts its will on the world and pursues his dreams. They also were the forbearers to four significant partnerships with men I had as an adult who taught me even more about masculinity.

The three Larrys along with Steve definitely helped me learn what the male psyche was all about, what makes guys different from girls and how to get along with them. I learned a lot in three years on that block about bows and arrows, cap pistols, playing marbles, and throwing dirt clods. But I can't really say they learned much in the way of dolls, jump rope or jacks from me, because they never wanted to play "girl stuff." That taught me a lot about the male ego of the 1950's. In a nutshell, most men wouldn't sacrifice their masculinity for any woman. Male intelligence is action orientated, dynamic, bold, and self-interested. And females are more naturally passive, receptive, compassionate and more interested in others. I was forced to accept maleness as equal even though their attitudes seemed contrary and foreign to the personality of my feminine soul. They often challenged me to hold onto the crown on my head and not give up my feminine qualities to elevate theirs. I lovingly embraced them as friends and they seemed to tolerate my interest in their world as they went about conquering it.

The three Larry's, Steve and I shared one big thing in common. We were all from single parent homes. In the mid 1950's, when *Father Knows Best* was the most popular television show and family values placed mother at home with the kids, we were exiled to play with each other as misfits lacking something that almost everyone else had, both parents' love. Larry and Steve across the street had no mother at home to nurture their male spirit. The other two Larry's up the street and myself had no father to protect us and teach us about achievement in the world. It seemed that someone or something had arranged us like dolls on a fabricated set to make a series of points.

Firstly, I realized that fate had produced a learning ground to bring maleness close to my heart, filling the void created by the absence of my father. With no father, who would normally offer a child examples of achievement, accomplishment, drive, and strength, the feminine soul gropes in the dark trying to find her masculine qualities without examples. It can be a difficult, if not an impossible, achievement without complementary mirrors to reflect on and learn from. Every woman must honor the male counterparts that come into her life as her teachers. She must see each one as bearing gifts, which promote her wholeness and show her an intelligence that increases hers. And conversely, it is difficult for men to honor womanhood without appreciating that the feminine characters in their life are offering them complementary qualities that complete them and nurture their spirit.

Secondly, sharing a common wound of abandonment with my four crowned princes helped me to identify, bond and move more compassionately toward others later in life. I realized early that the divine connection linking us together offered us a way to heal through our commonality. Throughout our lives we magnetize others who offer reflections of the early wounds which deny us love and which cast a shadow on our relationships. The light they shine on these wounds illuminates them so that they may eventually be released to the light of God.

Although none of the Larrys or Steves in my early childhood became my sweetheart at any time in my life, they did set the stage for the evolution of my soul to embrace the reflection of my inner masculine. Even at that young age, I was being prepared for the sacred marriage, the unification of the masculine and feminine within my soul. As early actors in my life's play, they appeared on stage and exited quickly, before the many acts and sequels that followed. All of my suitors, especially the four significant long term relationships taught me more about my capacity for love and reflected masculine attributes that brought me to wholeness.

At a pivotal time in my life, which I refer to as my spiritual emergence, four new characters walked on stage with me, three Lauras and a Stephanie. They immediately became my closest friends. Again there were four crowns, but now on the heads of feminine reflections who pointed me toward my authentic feminine soul. Each complemented me in a unique way with individual qualities of beauty, sensuality, intuition, and wisdom. And each arrived with a story line that would advance me out of the neglect and degradation of my feminine spirit and into appreciation for how a goddess should be treated.

By the time my Divine Complement came onto the stage, I was a mature queen ready for her king, a complement to share in a unique spiritual purpose to write. We were perfectly matched, my intuitive wisdom complementing his brilliance and style, and I was certain, at least for a time, that we could blend our strengths beautifully to write esoteric wisdom for the mainstream. But we never got that far. He fell in love with another woman and turned his back on our mutual destiny to forge a path of his own.

Much of the material for this book was collected over a period of a year. I set out each morning on a vision quest, a couple-hunting expedition that proved to create the most serendipitous meetings with couples in love that anyone could expect. Starbucks in Lahaina, Maui, was the site of a convention of honeymooners every day. The stories of magical first meetings between Divine Complements were so numerous that I had to carefully choose which ones to include in this book. In interviewing hundreds of couples, I can't remember one who didn't believe they were soul mates. Most said that it was love at first sight and that they felt they were swept along by a spiritual force that attracted and bonded them from the very beginning. Some met in grade school, others in college and many later in life—after failed marriages and raising children. No matter when or how they met, it was always relayed as if it was "meant to be." Some invisible force seemed to set the life stage for their partner's entrance. Most had no doubt that they would be together always, no matter what the divorce statistics said. Some had a strong sense that God was pulling them together while others said they had to pursue and convince their partner that they were the one. Some waited a long time for their complement to be free to begin anew with them and others were married in the first week. I heard stories of severe trials where complements had to overcome extraordinary problems such as near death experiences and stories of relationships that seemed to flow with opportunities from the get go. None of these people could imagine life without their complement, whether it was a roller coaster of ups and downs or a smooth sail, all that seemed to matter was that they were together.

Beyond their romantic ideals, their partner seemed to match them with what they couldn't draw out from within themselves. Most agreed that they were opposites—as different as night and day—and that seemed to work in keeping their partnership interesting and alive. Some were aware that their lives were a spiritual ground for learning lessons of love while others just shared their lives with little thought to the meaning. All agreed that relationship was hard work, but believed their partner was worth the effort.

Some I met were among the broken-hearted whose marriages failed despite their devotion and some were back together for a second chance. There were widows and widowers who couldn't imagine themselves with another partner. But even as they grieved their physical loss, they were still in communion with their complements within the heavenly dimensions, enough to keep the memories alive. Some couples were married for sixty years. Others were on their honeymoon, just beginning their life's journey together. All of them shared a common experience, a love that had grown from the moment they met and nourished their hearts and their relationship through whatever life presented them.

There is nothing more beautiful than to see a couple in their seventies walking hand and hand or with their arms around each other still sharing a romantic spark as if they were teenagers. I walked along side a number of them asking how they kept the passion fires aglow. They usually said they felt the same about each other as the first day they met. Nothing could stop the love they had for each other.

Even if you are a cynic who doesn't believe that soul

mates exist or someone who is disillusioned because you've been searching high and low for your perfect match and have not yet found them, you will agree that there is an other-worldly dimension to most of the stories that are sprinkled throughout this book. They may convert you into a born again believer in the concept of soul mates and in a divine destiny for two. Or they may merely cause you to reflect on all the divine experiences in life that seem unexplainable and magical.

Needless to say, there is a divine dimension to our existence that is penetrated when we fall in love, especially when that romantic encounter is with our Divine Complement. The veils are lifted for a time so that we may recognize the divine connection enough to take a chance at spiritual fulfillment with someone meant to complete and fulfill us. With our hearts and eyes open, we may even step consciously onto destiny's path appreciating the new life that has begun, one of complementary partnership that is meant to move us deeply into intimate arms.

The unfolding dream of life may offer each of us many chances at relationship to balance the scales in the heart, with the complementary male and female attributes that bring wholeness to the soul. But only a Divine Complement can offer the opportunity for that divine connection, completeness, and fullness, and that will balance the scales completely.

Divine Principle:

Wherever it is that we first and finally meet our Divine Complement, it will forever be known as divine territory.

Chapter 1

Meant To Be

Divine Principle:
Divine Complements harmonize a field of creative potential to perform miracles of God's power. Their meeting is the first of those miracles.

*T*he meeting of Divine Complements can be a magical event that points a couple directly toward each other's heart and to the memory of an earlier soul-to-soul connection. The attraction goes beyond a biological urge to mate and procreate and is more than a chemistry of sniffs and smells and sex appeal. It also goes beyond the reasoning "He or she suits me," in which case we are fulfilling a personal ideal.

Sizing up our soul mate as a potential partner is not an

intellectual task. We must succumb to the magnetic attraction, a harmony of spiritual collaboration that is perfectly
orchestrated in the moment. This harmony is magnetic, mysterious, entrancing, enchanting and otherworldly. It forces us
to take note of the radiant light of the other and the brighter
light we create together. We move deeply into a soulful place
reminding us of an altogether different place and time, where
unity was a given and we were free to dance together in the
harmony of God's love. Though we are still asleep to the
details of the real promise and the destiny we co-created long
before, for this one moment in time we are awakened to
something in our heart that says this is someone special to
appreciate. It may even be love at first sight.

From there, hours of conversation may follow, ushering
us into familiar places as soul memories trickle in. We may
feel that we have known each other's face, warmth and soul
forever. It is true. We are old friends indeed, soulful friends
and kindred spirits who waltzed together through many lifetimes. It is likely we shared numerous lifetimes, in which we
grew to know each other's essence more and more intimately. Although our individual personalities are different from
one lifetime to the next, the soul of our beloved has a common place in our heart. We have only chosen veils of appearance and personality to hide our identities from each other in
this life so we can begin anew the tests of love. Now, only a
faint inkling of familiarity remains.

There may be a great deal of serendipity and the magic of
synchronicity to convince us that this person is divinely connected to us. Perhaps we lived on the same block or around
the corner for the last four years without realizing it and now
we meet under a movie marquee that reads "Soul Mate." The
last four digits of our phone numbers may be the same or we
may have had the same locker number in high school. One

may drive a red Mustang with white interior, while the other drives a white Mustang with red interior. Both our parents might have an aunt in Philadelphia named Mary. We may have twin names like Joe and Josie or Earnest and Ernestine (a phenomenon I have run into more than once). What is even more likely is that we share some of the same interests, complementary talents and visions for the future.

This serendipity may bring us to laughter or to tears, to magical thinking and wondering if God is near. We may consider whether this was "meant to be." "Am I the one for him, or is she the one for me?" "Where will we go from here?"

Most of the time, these questions can't be answered with certainty until the heart is secure in knowing that this meeting was definitely meant to be. It may take considerable time, courage, and exploration to affirm the divine connection. For some, the affirmation will come in an instant, and for others the confirmation could take months or years.

Ordinary logic, however, may deny us the opportunity to solidify the synchronicities and serendipity into a meaningful event of lasting significance. It may even dismiss all the magical evidence as sheer coincidence, luck or just plain nonsense. Logic seldom agrees with the heart. In fact, it may chase away the pangs of the heart to maintain some sanity and control. Those who bend to their logical minds may not recognize the spiritual power behind all the miracles that are pulling them toward their Divine Complements. For them, their soul mates remain strangers, just another possibility among thousands.

It is the true spiritual power and combined destiny of Divine Complements that move mountains and clear the path to bring two souls together. Both hearts wish to explore each other as a deeply connected couple, who has reunited after a long absence. The mind will either accept and embrace this profound experience or compromise it by inciting fear, suspicion or denial. It is this push-pull between the mind and the heart that must end in order for the promise between Divine Complements to be fulfilled. The heart must win the battle for love, with the mind surrendering to the knowing that the deliverance of divine complementary partnership was "meant to be."

I struck up a conversation with a young woman while sipping coffee at Starbucks who shared a dream that shed some light on the authenticity of her soul mate. She and her boyfriend were friends for five years before embarking on a romantic relationship. She told me she wasn't at all sure that he was the "one" or that she could trust him despite the fact that he had always proved faithful and honest.

In her dream, she was with her spiritual teacher, and another young woman, who appeared to be lost and confused. The perplexed dream character turned out to be confused about what town she was in, though she had some sense that she was in Italy. She asked, "Am I in Rome or somewhere else?" The spiritual teacher showed her on a map that she was in Verona, Italy. She pointed out the streets and sites that surrounded her and commented that they should appear familiar. Both the dreamer and the lost woman exclaimed "Aha!" I asked the dreamer what she associated with Verona and she told me that she had visited there when she was in her 20s and that she considered it romantic and beautiful. She thought that perhaps the dream was pointing to the famous lovers Romeo and Juliet, as Shakespeare's play is set in Verona. I intuited immediately that her subconscious was letting her know she had found her soul mate. With her mental chatter and doubts, she was denying recognition of the authenticity of their connection. The spiritual guide was pointing to this juncture in her life as an opportunity for commitment between soul-mate lovers who, like

Romeo and Juliet, would sacrifice everything to be together. The dream was meant to illuminate her—she just needed some help in understanding what it meant. After I gave her an intuitive reading that revealed why she had delayed recognizing the authenticity of her soulmate, she seemed convinced that less processing and more plunging might be in order.

Divine Complements' personal stories are heartwarming and amazing, full of twists and turns and magical events that finally brought them to each other's arms. For some lucky people, the journey begins with their first love. Perhaps as high school sweethearts who know they need not play the field for very long. These early bonds can last a lifetime. As divine partners, they need all the time in the world to spiritually develop within a sacred relationship. Neither could do as well apart in learning life's intended lessons. It is likely that they will have children to parent in the future to whom they owe a great deal because they transgressed in some way in a previous lifetime. For these couples, their relationship is meant to be a lifelong spiritual path along on which they will help each other grow spiritually and humanly over decades. They are meant to awaken to God's love together and move to deeper and deeper levels of friendship and love. They may succeed or they may fail, but their relationship is meant to be a lasting one.

Just this afternoon, I saw a couple kissing in front of a mall near my home. I approached the young woman after her partner had gone into the mall while she waited on a bench outside. I said, "You look so much in love." She smiled, blushed a bit and said she and her husband were on their honeymoon. I asked her whether the day they met was a magical experience. She said, "Oh yes." She was only 15 and her husband was barely 16 the day they met at church during her confirmation ceremony. "It was such a spiritual experience, and we have been together ever since, looking forward to our wedding day." I asked whether she believed it was meant to be. Her answer was an unequivocal "yes."

Their courtship lasted 13 years before they finally tied the knot. They had decided to first to finish college and to earn some money to share the expense of the wedding with her family. Whatever the case, their love stood the test of a long engagement and they were ready to open another chapter of their divine journey together.

Weddings seem to inspire other weddings. Several complements I have met were attending friends' weddings when they met. In fact, I recently read that two of the Dixie Chicks met their husbands at weddings. I spoke to a couple standing in line at Taco Bell who were planning on being married the next day in a lush-paradise setting under a waterfall. The young man joked that they were tired of luxurious dinners on Maui, being waited on and treated special, so they decided on Taco Bell for their prenuptial dinner. When I asked how they'd met, he told me it was at a wedding where he was the best man and she was a maid of honor. They connected that day in the landscape of spiritual love between two close friends and knew immediately that they, too, were meant for each other. They became engaged Nov. 10th the same year and set the wedding date for four years later to the day.

Seemingly happenstance meetings are not happenstance at all but part of a co-creative plan to bring two together in such a sacred and meaningful way that they can never forget the importance of the day they met. No one can deny how romantic and meaningful it would be to meet your future husband or wife at another's wedding. Two souls could never have designed a more spiritually oriented encounter, listening to the nuptial vows recited on the day they met. The memory would be indelibly etched in their hearts and minds forever. To everyone around them who might witness their reunion, they are reminded also that there is a thing called destiny and divine timing.

The magical way in which a couple meet signals to their hearts to embrace each other as the most significant person to have entered their lives. They are not likely to dismiss the significance of the other without a struggle when their destiny is upon them like this. Even if they are not completely cognizant of the information in their hearts, they will recognize the magical events that brought them together as meaningful. Because these magical meetings are more like something out of a romantic comedy, non-ordinary, mystical and godly, we might refer to them as "spiritual romantic encounters of the third kind"; they are inexplicable in ordinary terms and otherworldly in their origins.

When we encounter our soul mate, we are shot out of the ordinary world and into the dimensions of our spiritual nature. Our hearts open to an awareness of the spiritual force within and behind the miracles around us. We ascend to divine territory. We might think, "God delivered my beloved to my door." Or, "He or she was heaven-sent." The heavenly dimension at work is a field of harmony beyond our view. It is a dimension of co-creative design that harmonizes and manifests a "meant to be" reunion on the physical plane. Within this field, the spiritual force of the beloved embraces us. Love abounds and grace follows as we explore this divine connection day after day. We may hesitate in confusion for a while, but we will inevitably be pushed onto the path of destiny together. Call it fate or kismet. It was certain to happen.

Hopefully, we will learn in time that the magical meeting was a sacred event to help us understand the scope of a spiritually bonded relationship. And if the memory of this first encounter sticks like glue and we don't let our mind sabotage it, we will be bonded through this experience for months and years to come. By holding the sacredness of that day in our hearts, no matter what challenges we face or what disagreements we have in the future, we will return to honoring our soul mate again.

A friend recently told me about a happily-ever-after complement story that is one of the most magical and serendipitous meetings I have heard about. It is a story of two complements that met on the heavenly web, the Internet. The woman was planning a trip to New Zealand and visited a New Zealand chat room to get suggestions on what to see and where to eat. She struck up a conversation with a man who she thought lived in New Zealand, and they immediately hit it off. After a little e-mailing back and forth, it came out that the man lived three blocks from her. He had previously lived in New Zealand and was fond of the chat room. They arranged to meet and are now happily exploring their "meant to be" relationship. They traveled to New Zealand together, their holy ground, within a month of their meeting.

The reunion of Divine Complements is no more happenstance than the birth of a child they may have in the future. All souls collaborate spiritually within soul groups to join us in life as close family members and kindred friends. Our own soul groups, or spiritual brethren, have traveled alongside us over many lifetimes. They have offered the keys to spiritual growth in each of these lifetimes, able to teach us about meaningful friendships, boundaries, compassion and other spiritual human achievements. Invited or not, they are our teachers, here to help us unravel the patterns of a creative legacy, helping to change our hearts, and paving the way for our future. They bring with them lessons of love and help us to balance the karma we have accumulated with them. Our failings with each other in previous lifetimes determine the

fate we have together in this lifetime. Some karmic alliances will become lasting friendships that we can learn to honor for what they bring us. Others come and go quickly, brief encounters that complete the karma from a previous life. Some pose difficult tests and represent less-perfect ideals than the ones we may wish for. Still others, like our children, are here to just love us innocently and offer us opportunities to love them back with respect and commitment. Soul journeyers enter our life at the perfect evolutionary moment. It seems as if they need a reciprocal lesson from us at that same moment in time. Our lessons together represent our evolutionary plan for personal development. We have a karmic contract to improve each other that must be honored.

Our Divine Complement may be the first of many or the last to arrive with whom we have a karmic contract. They arrive with the distinction of having the longest-standing karmic history with us. Our complement is meant to remain committed to us through every lesson of love and test of fate. However, no one can give us an ironclad guarantee that they will be mature enough to commit for the long haul. Whether we make it to the altar or even last a month will depend on our willingness to embrace, accept and bond to our beloved.

Divine Principle:
A destiny is inscribed in the heart and eternal soul of man.

"Meant to be" is just another term for destiny. No matter what we were told or what we may believe about our individual choices, our life has an underlying meaningful plan. We call this plan destiny. Although there are some strong, intelligent voices that are clearly against the notion that a destiny that is predetermined even exists, a destiny is inscribed in the heart and eternal soul of man.

Destiny is of our soul's making, not determined by our mind or the desire to have everything we think we want. Although we can forge ahead with plans of our own, some very well-thought-out and devised to achieve comfort or success as measured by cultural standards, our soul is nudging us forward on its own unique evolutionary plan for spiritual achievement. This plan may support our personal design or it may contradict it, giving us instead exactly what we need to grow in consciousness, not necessarily what we want materially. We call it fate's helping hand.

Fate is a universal law and cosmic principle that offers us our just due, what we deserve as opposed to what we think we deserve. The Greeks have a beautiful name for fate, Moira, the cosmic principle of binding apportionment. Moira selects and distributes our "due portion" in life, whether it is in the form of financial opportunities or opportunities for loving friendships.

Fate grants us our due in reaction to our previous acts of free will. The reaction can be immediate or it can follow us for thousands of lifetimes. What goes around eventually comes around. Therefore, even if we consistently choose love over hatred and live a moral life, we are not guaranteed a blissful life with everything we want with our Divine Complement. We may instead experience years of limitation and hardships that make us wonder, "Why us?" In truth, because we failed lifetimes before, we had chosen these limitations just before our incarnations so that our souls and our relationship could mature.

Destiny unfolds creatively, putting in front of us the tasks our soul has decided to accomplish in this life. It offers many opportunities for growth, connecting us with people who are there to hold our hand, slap our hand or lead our hand toward giving more of ourselves, like our love, compassion or a helping hand. If we fail to adopt a virtue or a spiritual principle and instead fall to jealousy or hatred, fate will give us important lessons so that we may improve ourselves. We may have to make amends with those we harmed in past lives and move toward higher understanding and respect for them and our relationship to them in this life. We choose, we grow or we lose. Again and again, lifetime after lifetime, our plan evolves because our higher self demands more perfection.

We are offered glimpses of our potentials on the path of our destiny. Potentials of greatness that we may only aspire to now but can achieve with the right dose of help. Many people arrive in our life like characters in a movie, reflecting qualities that we ourselves may need to develop within our own personality. They, like all of us, have successes and failures to their name, special talents and achievements and ways of approaching life that bring a sense of personal fulfillment. Our friends' characteristics and talents are like jewels of different radiant qualities for us to try on and appreciate. If they glisten in our heart, we can wear them proudly. Complements on the path promote our wholeness and improve our character and our life, should we learn from their example. Friends may also mimic the attitudes and beliefs we hold in our mind. They are mirrors reflecting good and bad mind-sets and their behaviors may at times appall us. If someone in our circle of friends cheats on a spouse, we may very well judge him for a grave mistake we would never want to make. Yes, we may have been tempted in the past, but the consequences to their family life may affirm that fidelity will always be our chosen path. If someone we know has had emotional difficulties because of trauma experienced in childhood, he may point us to the wounded child within our own heart. In communicating about their pain and history, we may be driven back to own early experiences so that the memories can be excavated and brought into the light. Through a process of identification, we may become more compassionate toward ourselves and with those who have lived with the same kind of emotional pain. Embracing others' reflections helps us to witness ourselves more fully and accurately and to define who we are. We may need to retrieve parts of our authentic selves that have been abandoned or denied as they are revealed to us through the reflecting mirror. Every piece complements our authentic core and helps to complete us. Our destiny path leads us to each and every one of the complementary pieces of the complex puzzle of our soul. We can embrace the characters in the story about us or turn away without opening the gifts they give.

Our own Divine Complement will meet us on the path of destiny holding that largest piece for us to admire, embrace and cherish. He or she will mirror our own masculine or feminine side. If a man, he will offer masculine traits as examples. Perhaps he is hard-working, focused, strong and talented. We may wish we were as brilliant or courageous. Inside we are, as our qualities are undeveloped or underdeveloped only for a time. Our complement's example will help us bring forth those qualities from within ourselves. If a woman, our complement may offer us entrance to the emotional side of life, teaching us how to be compassionate, nurturing and intuitive. She may show us how to follow our hunches, how to make friends and keep them and how to nurture ourselves through self-love and self-acceptance. Polished, perfect or not, our complement is likely to hold the very talents and authentic qualities we must develop. Our task will be to become more like each other without giving up the authentic qualities we each have. The process may take considerable time and effort. Although we will always maintain our uniqueness, we will grow toward improving our character and balancing the harmonies of our soul. The masculine and feminine aspects will one day dance in a complete harmony of power as we become more integrated through the constant reflection of our partner.

Destiny spreads out before us in every moment, urging us to follow its course with curiosity, an open mind and an open heart. It can be approached with the excitement and wonder of a child who has opened the doors to the magic kingdom or it can be avoided altogether because of uncertainty and fear of the unknown. Our destiny is manifested through our intention and willingness to step boldly onto its path. When the relationship with our Divine Complement is before us, we may be asked to shed the fears and masks that deny us love and to step beside the person who can love us. Our path will no longer be a solitary one without companionship and support but rather a path of unity and synergistic experiences that offer us fulfillment time and time again.

Our destiny is merely an outline of each chapter of our life. To fulfill the tasks we have been given, we need only to creatively write the details. Each chapter may have a heading such as "the lesson of forgiveness" or "the lesson of greed." The chapter opens with our complement as our leading man or woman, and we begin to weave our story together, hopefully appreciating the experiences that teach us these important lessons. Many characters will arrive to play out their parts and fulfill their roles in our lives. We all collaborate to write the stories of our lives together, each helping to fulfill the destiny of the other. There will be romance, adventure, comedy and mystery. When one chapter closes, another opens, moving us into a new phase of life. Each phase offers new potentials and opportunities for the growth of our human soul.

Our destiny with our soul mate is not likely to be revealed to us as a map or guide spelling out times, places and events, though we might wish we had a manual advising us how to cope with their idiosyncrasies. Accurately reading our complement's personality will be an intuitive process of investigation that could take years of development. We will learn through experience just what makes them happy and what encourages them to grow and to become more intimate with us.

Our destiny with our complement is like a mutual dream we dreamed together. This dream will have signs that will become meaningful clues to the spiritual power behind the relationship. The synchronicities and signs in life, which offer information about our destiny, can be interpreted much like the material in our night dreams whose meaning may bring us food for thought. Clues are often hidden in the details of our life, and unless we are awake intuitively, they may not register in our mind as anything significant.

The term "synchronicity" refers to an event or circumstance that is magical and meaningful—a meaningful coincidence. A girlfriend called me with a funny synchronicity that happened between her and her partner recently. Early in the morning, his car's fan belt broke, and he had to spend the afternoon fixing it. A couple of hours later, while she was vacuuming the carpet, the belt to the beater bar broke. She called me immediately for an interpretation. As both the fan belt and the vacuum belt unify two parts to make the motor purr and the machine function, so too does it take a love connection to unify two hearts. In this case, two people had broken their connection in some way. As we explored the day's events, she acknowledged that they had recently had some miscommunications that resulted in emotional distance and led her to doubt his devotion to her. The meaningful synchronicity of both belts breaking was pointing out the problem. Broken connections need an opportunity to mend. "Stop what you're doing and sort things out now," the broken belts were saying.

Synchronicities offer a trail of clues to what is hidden in the field of the elaborate tapestry of our soul's design. As signs, they may capture our attention when we least expect a message. It may be felt only as an inkling of something just around the corner, or it may be so obvious that we can't ignore it. These indicators on the path of our destiny bring meaning to our existence and connect us to our own higher intelligence, which guides the way.

Just a few moments ago, I stepped out onto my moonlit porch and looked into the horizon. A beautiful moonbow was cresting as a white shimmering arch against the night sky. Moonbows, also known as lunar rainbows, are extremely rare and seemingly magical occurrences. In fact, I remember seeing only one other. Just last night, after admiring the full moon, one of the members of my dream group told me she wished she would see a moonbow, as she never has. Last night's conversation tied the knot in the creative plan for today and prophesied the moonbow. As a sign, it holds a promise of fulfillment.

Synchronicities can appear like heaven-sent messages about the future we have planned with our soul mate. They most often aren't recognized or understood until after the fact, but when we begin to compare notes, we may discover that destiny was leaving a trail of clues years before.

I am reminded of a beautiful story told to me by a woman who had some clues early on about the man she would marry. She said that when she was about 16 years old she was riding in the car with her father and passed a billboard that had the name of a man who was running for public office. The name was an unusual French name that seemed to jump out toward her. She thought at the time that it was the weirdest and most repulsive-sounding name she had ever heard. Little did she know that she would meet her Divine Complement five years later, marry him and have to take that repulsive-sounding name as her own.

Another couple I met recently told me about their courageous destiny story. They were Yugoslavian refugees who separately fled Bosnia and immigrated to the U.S. in 1999. She landed in Twin Falls, Idaho, and he in Boise to join family members and close friends. A friend of the young man's father said, "I have the perfect match for you." He invited the young man to Twin Falls to meet her. He made two trips to Twin Falls to meet the mystery girl, but both times, for one reason or another, she was not available for a date. However, his father's friend persisted and encouraged the young man to return. The third time proved to be the charm. They finally met and began to date. During their courtship, he drove almost 300 miles every week to Twin Falls to take her out, sometimes driving back to Boise with her the same day. They were married within four months of their meeting and said it was kismet. I couldn't help but wonder how may times the young man had passed highway signs reading "Twin Falls" on the way to court his "twin," or Divine Complement. Twin Falls was a metaphoric and geographical sign offering a clue that fate was weaving a mutual destiny for this couple, 'twin souls' who had perhaps fallen lifetimes before. Neither of them had recognized it until I pointed out the dream logic. They laughed a belly laugh with me about life's synchronicities.

Night dreams are another way of retrieving some of our destiny's bigger picture. I remember having a dream five years before I met my Divine Complement. In the dream, I was sitting at the breakfast table with Mel Gibson and was straddling his lap acting flirtatious and playful. I asked him for a commitment, but he appeared nervous and taken aback by my boldness. He said he wasn't sure he could commit. He said, "Japanese men don't commit, do they?" At the time, I thought Mel to be truly the archetype of the ideal male whose attributes as a successful and accomplished actor were reflective of my own male side. Fame was on the drawing board in my thoughts and pursuits. And as a result, my interpretation, I confess, was way off base. I thought of Mel's role as the hero in *Braveheart*, fighting for freedom and his homeland. The archetype suited my own personality, questing for spiritual enlightenment and toward fulfilling my higher purpose. Admittedly, I needed to develop my masculine side a bit more to forge forward with my destiny and thought the dream was telling me I needed to make a greater commitment to my spiritual mission. It wasn't until much later, after my Divine Complement entered my life, that I realized he was the Mel Gibson in my dream—someone who complemented me, but who was not going to commit to me. The comment about Japanese men characterized a conservative patriarchal personality type whose thinking was dominated by business, an archetype reflecting my complement's desire for self-fulfillment.

The dream offered me a glimpse of what was to come five years later. Though no preparation of my heart could have sufficiently bolstered me for such a disappointment, I should have known from the revealing material in my dream that I would be confronted with circumstances that were less than my ideal.

Synchronicities and dreams can offer important clues that point to the identity and significance of our "meant to be" partner. They emerge out of the co-creative field, the playground of twin souls' making, revealing elements of a future that is on the drawing board. They may manifest like a rainbow on a cloudy day offering a promise of fulfillment in the horizon. Dreams, like the one I had, offer proof that a divine destiny between soul mates exists, orchestrated in a dimension of the soul beyond our normal consciousness. Through recognizing and appreciating our dreams, we can step onto the path of destiny consciously and gain insight into some of the challenges that may be presented later. Our mutual dream with our complement will be fulfilled through our conscious choice to commit to the creative design of our destiny and to embrace the miracles that bring us together.

Divine Principle:
Free will, destiny and fate are synergizers of life's course. With our Divine Complement before us, we are at destiny's door and in fate's arms. And it is our free will that will determine whether we walk through destiny's door together, appreciating and accepting the arms that fate has placed us in.

The story line of a divine destiny will be presented in life chapters, some of which will bring fulfillment while others challenge the heart emotionally. Undoubtedly, a chapter ended right before our Divine Complement entered our life. We may have made commitments within a previous relationship, met them or betrayed our pledge. If we failed miserably, we will undoubtedly have karma to resolve, like a pile of financial debt. The weight of one partner's karma will be felt by the other and may pose limitations on what they can achieve together.

I am reminded of an old Sufi story about the mouse that married an elephant. The elephant died suddenly, and little did the mouse know that its destiny was to spend the rest of its life digging a hole for its beloved's grave. Though difficult to swallow, the poetic vows "in sickness and in health, for richer or for poorer" are reality-based. Limitations on our lives put love to the test. Our willingness to embrace every bit of good and a little of the bad will honor us in the end and support the path of our sacred relationship. The hard times will turn into better times if we have learned from our mistakes, forgiven ourselves and let go of the pain. Our path is cleared and our life filled with new creative potentials when we confront the past and complete the karma we carried over from previous relationships in this life.

Although we are destined to meet our divine partner and the others who are meant to improve us, we are 100 percent free to choose in every moment to love them or to abandon our promises to them. Choice is a part of the human experience, and conscious choices further our evolution, awarding more freedom. Ignorance and unconsciousness lead us toward limitations, mistrust and loss. We are always completely free to choose love or hatred, generosity or greed, commitment or abandonment in each and every moment of our life. The choice to commit to our Divine Complement, honoring our soul's promise and purpose, may be the greatest test we have to face in our life.

Our free will most surely create our fate. Fate is not cast down by God as punishment but created by our own soul for our highest good so that we can attain the consciousness of God. We are certain to suffer every time we neglect the path of love that God is. Time and time again, we will feel the karmic repercussions as limitations in our physical world should we stray. Our fate may arise from our immediate actions, or it may have been determined by previous life-times. Karmic repercussions are brought to us as improve-ment lessons that will slap us in the face in hopes of hum-bling us at God's door. Through suffering we are brought to humility and into recognition of the divine principles that guide humanity. Suffering offers us the choice to love.

With our Divine Complement before us, we are at des-tiny's door and in fate's arms. And it is our free will that will determine whether we walk through destiny's door together, appreciating and accepting the arms that fate opened for us. Henry Miller said it perfectly: "Destiny is what you are sup-posed to do in life. Fate is what kicks you in the ass to do it." As most of us know, the challenges of a new relationship are apt to kick us in the ass at least once or twice.

Our soul urges us to move onto the path of our destiny, consciously pursuing the opportunities to become enlight-ened to love. Love is the bottom-line foundation in every area of life. To know its meaning and its grace is something that is attainable. People may pursue many things that they believe will fulfill them and give value to their existence. Sometimes the struggle for significance can lead us onto a path to honor ourselves while denying others. Our life unfolds to the cred-it and benefit of each soul who is a part of our spiritual des-tiny. We may be ushered into it with loving hands from some-one who has traveled the path before us, and we will both benefit from that loving action. Our Divine Complement may be the very one to open the doors of consciousness into the spiritual realms of God, or we may be the one to lead them.

Our soul's creative destiny can be put on the back burner or completely incinerated in each life depending on our free choices. Hopefully, we will be enlightened enough to make choices that benefit those who walk beside us as well as choices that benefit ourselves. Embracing our Divine

Complement when the curtain rises and they are standing onstage will be the most important choice we make in our life. It will begin a life for two who were meant to be in communion, setting the stage for future acts of love.

Though parts of our destiny are inscribed within our hearts, whether and how we get to our destination in this life is of our making. We set our intention and vision for the future, get into the car and hopefully share the driving duties with our complement. Those who know how to lead as well as follow will end up at their destination with less difficulty. It is through the synergistic balance of equality in partnership that the creative design will come into form.

Nothing should keep our complementary relationship from being given every opportunity to begin on the right foot. We are destined to move in tandem with our beloved, forging up hill on a bicycle meant for two and coasting at those times when we are in sync with God's love.

Divine Principle:
The illumination of God is our ultimate destiny. It is achieved through a transition that sheds the singular life that we hold so meaningful and brings us to a sacred union with the divine.

Each person's destiny is a soul's quest to reach greater potentials of love. To know that love is the essence through which we grow and evolve spiritually and humanly brings meaning to our existence. Our personal quest for love brings with it many experiences that expand our capacity for love and coax us to express love to others. We should arrive at an understanding of God's love for us and renew our love for

God. The more love we give through service, the more likely we are to become enlightened.

Enlightenment is the state of at-oneness with God and every particle of God's expression on Earth. It is a clear state of spiritual love that expands the heart and unifies our consciousness with the Creator. Within this state we can reach for the stars and find God's vibration in every blade of grass beneath our feet. The divine truth is that God's creative pulse lives in all the layers or dimensions of existence in our universe. God is in nature, the air we breathe, and in the convenience store around the corner. As Jesus told his disciples, "The kingdom of the father is spread out upon the earth, and men do not see it."

There is a time of spiritual emergence, when we may open to the creative power and higher intelligence of our God-self, even attaining states of enlightenment and self-realization. This time is known as a spiritual quickening or awakening. We may move beyond the boundaries of our world of limitations and open to the miracles of manifestation that the enlightened path has in store. Our Divine Complement may be the catalyst of initiation into these dimensions of God. The unified harmony of beloveds creates the power of God and activates the higher mind. When touched deeply and intimately by our beloved, we enter the field of God, surrendering to the love that is offered. Love accelerates and awakens our spirit to expand into dimensions of the divine. This experience of divine ecstasy will push us out of the ordinary conditioning of our human dimension and into the pure light of God.

The love between Divine Complements is a dimension of God's love. We love more and fear less with each step we take into that dimension. The experiences of love with our complement offer us opportunities to illuminate the places in our hearts that still need tending. For some, their Divine

Complement may enter at that perfect evolutionary moment and escort them through the door to a spiritual life. Before that life can be entered, the darkness must be illuminated and our ego must surrender. Our complement may light the darkness to reveal the scars that can ultimately be healed through his or her love. Once the miracle has been accomplished, they can help us surrender to be reborn to our own inner light, the creative intelligence locked deep within our hearts. We will blossom into the creative potentials that electrify life and humble us with the knowledge that we are one with God as well as with our beloved.

The reunification with God is the furthest point on our destiny path, the ultimate illumination and communion with the one source of everything. Whether we meet God in death or through enlightenment depends on how far our soul has evolved in each life or incarnation through service to love. Before we can meet our maker, we must take a stab at love on this earthly plane time and time again in hopes of renewing love again and again. To love ourselves, in a beautiful expression of godliness, wins us the first prize. To stand humble in naked innocence, having let go of the karma, shame, self— blame and hatred, will bring us to God's door. We must cast aside false faces in favor of our authentic self. It is not an easy accomplishment, but our Divine Complement and other members of our soul group are there to give us a hand. Our greatest prize comes in bringing our divine partner with us, helping his or her soul evolve alongside ours to complete the lessons of forgiveness, respect and love that we have chosen to co-create through committed relationship. We are offered a chance to author life together with a pure intention and an open heart. It is our choice whether to remain open to the power of love in each moment of our lives.

Chapter 2

The Stellar Promise

Divine Principle:
Twin Souls are bound together through a signature within their
hearts. The love between them is everlasting.

*T*he sacred union between Divine Comple-
ments has origins beyond this sphere of earthly embodiment.
The match was made in heaven. The creation of souls as stellar angels was a creative miracle that occurred long before the
creation of Adamic Man and the physical reality we call earth.
The human soul and spirit was birthed in a fluid of love, pre-
ceding time and space and the spheres of our known universe. We were created within an infinite realm of a divine
source we know as God, in a paradise of milk and honey, a
life-giving love and energy. It wasn't an earthly paradise but
an otherworldly field of light and love that stretches through
infinite space—beyond the beyond.

God breathed into existence a multitude of souls who reflected the essence of God's most beautiful expressions. We were all radiant beings of light harmonies that could move through the creative fluids of God's light, in continued communion with God and each other. As children set free on a playground, we were the joy in the Creator's eyes and examples of his/her power to love and put into form and existence beautiful souls as children, daughters and sons of light. What God conceived was a miracle of beauty, bounty, intelligence and love that could multiply beyond the beyond and spread love and creativity everywhere. Out of God's heart and in God's mind we were conceived in his/her image and essence. God made us uniquely creative, beautiful, intelligent and bold. We were all creatively perfect in the beginning.

Within God's plan was a beautiful promise, that each soul would be joined to a perfect stellar complement with whom he or she would be spiritually bound and forever unified. In the beginning, God created twin souls, not singular individual souls who had no one to play with. God created two together who would be the example of the love that God wished to be propagated everywhere and forever. Two who would be in communion with each other and with God always. The Creator birthed them along with other soul twins within huge soul groups—spiritual brethren.

The twin souls or "stellar twins" were linked through a beautiful template of love within the Stellar Heart, a significant masterpiece at the center of the fabric of the oversoul. Within this chasm of the Stellar Heart, stellar twins would be forever harmonized, no matter how far apart their souls might travel. The harmony of one was locked into the heart of the other in spirit and fused by love. And when creatively together in purpose and intention, they created a magnification of God's love everywhere they traveled.

Each individual soul was made of radiant harmonies that were different yet complementary to others'. Complete and whole within itself, each soul had both male and female aspects. Each soul was therefore androgynous. The unified creative intelligence of both male and female harmonies within each soul was a perfect intelligent design and a reflection of God's unified intelligence. The masculine angular, brilliant intelligence that was the active creative principle abounded with glory and higher intelligence. The feminine receptive, intuitive and emotional side was pure wisdom. These two light harmonies intertwined in a unified dance of everlasting creative intelligence in spirit form. They were equal in power and intelligence and yet different, the way colors have different hues and melodies have different notes. These harmonies were unified into a complex matrix and web of light that was crystalline in structure and made up the complete design of the Stellar Body—a God Suit.

Much like the intricate and individual design of a snowflake, the matrix for each individual soul was a unique coded design with distinct individual attributes and characteristics. Each soul was both god/goddess blooming with the radiant attributes of the individual matrix God had chosen for them. This unified essence is still locked indelibly within the oversoul DNA and within the human form as spirit.

We can look to the structure of the double helix spiral of the human DNA to find biological evidence of a binary nature in the primary structure of human biology. Two strands of DNA intertwine in a spiral ladder, with a multitude of genes and message sequences coded in pairs. There are some 35,000 genes arranged on the DNA molecule comprising chemical bases arranged in approximately three billion precise sequences. They carry a digital code of information and messages, which represent a special language about the individual and its traits. This binary nature of the human form is only one aspect of how the human form of Adamic Man was programmed. The oversoul has a DNA structure that is far more complex than the DNA at the biological level. Instead of two strands, twelve strands are intertwined in a language of light. The oversoul is the connection of the human form to the Creator.

We can better understand our imprinted connection to God by applying numerology to the meaning of the twelve strands. The number 12 may be reduced to the number 3 as "1 + 2 = 3." This trinity represents the unity of the male and female polarities and the One Absolute, forming a creative matrix of God/ Goddess power. We might imagine that the intelligence of the higher self, with its 12 strands, is far greater than the intelligence of the third-dimensional mind, with its two strands.

What are the creative potentials in having a 12-strand DNA code? They are vast and limitless creative potentials of a higher intelligence that are beyond human comprehension at the physical, material level. Jesus Christ was one living example of a realized and transfigured Stellar Angel, God manifest. The miracles of manifestation that Jesus created in healing the sick and feeding the multitudes, along with his supernatural clairvoyant knowledge of the future, are small examples of what each individual soul is capable of achieving, should spiritual evolution bring them to this destiny.

The binary dance of the male and female polarities coupled with the push of God's grace has the creative potential and intelligence to create spheres and worlds of its own. However, we have been locked in a universe of duality and separation that limits our ascension to our Stellar Soul's limitless potentials. No one standing on Earth's sphere has attained the kind of power to transfigure this world and create a new one. However, many have achieved enlightened states and empowered themselves to create small miracles within a limited field of manifestation. In fact, the co-creative design between twin souls creates their reunion through this field of harmony. Synchronicities and serendipitous experiences are the result of the creative experience of this unified intelligence on a creative field known as the fifth dimension. Within this fifth dimension, thoughts, desires and intentions bring manifestations of opportunity through the door. We think it and there it is. The fifth dimension also offers us lessons of limitation that challenge us to grow in increments toward a better understanding of the creative laws of the universe and push us to apply the ingredient of love in every situation. Though many have achieved enlightened states and ascended in their consciousness beyond the third dimension, the Kingdom of God remains unrealized, still locked within the matrix of the Stellar Heart. As Jesus reminded us, the Kingdom of God is within.

For many, a transformation and rebirth of the soul to embody its androgyny may be the first step in realizing some of the potentials of the oversoul. For example, I had a transformational dream many years ago in which I gave birth to a cherub-faced child with both male and female genitalia. The dream illuminated my soul's androgyny and ushered in creative potentials that expanded my consciousness.

The true face of God seems unknowable, except to those whose innocence makes them worthy to be God's messengers. I came to better understand the unified nature of God when my daughter, who was six at the time, drew me a beautiful picture of God. I had often pondered what God really looked like after I had rejected the classical patriarchal images of The Father, who sat in the heavens commanding honor and obedience. The patriarchal image is far from what my daughter envisioned. She drew a large circle of golden light in the sky that took up most of the background of the picture. The circle was divided in half. She had labeled one side "boy," the other side "girl." The entire circle of golden light she had labeled "God." Above the circle was a sun in the right-hand corner and a moon in the upper left. The sun and the moon each had long arms that reached across the paper toward each other as if they were attempting to grasp each other's intelligence. The symbolism of the sun and the moon represents the lunar and solar aspects within the human soul, the male and female polarities. The arms reaching across the sky I saw as the polarities' attempt to traverse the heavens to embrace in a sacred union. With a voice of authority, my daughter announced that she had communicated with God. "Mommy, God told me to tell you that you have to turn all your power over to God". At the time I had been going through a great deal of emotional turmoil over allowing my daughter to resume visitation with her father. Although I had sole custody, he had regained visitation rights after a year without them. I thought it was within my power to use ritual and magic to make sure she didn't have to see him. Before resorting to that, I received the command from God through the innocent mouthpiece of my daughter. She taught me that God's power should not be used to manipulate events, which in this case were fate's karmic lessons among father, daughter and mother. I learned there is a creative design, a perfect plan being set into motion that was blessed by God for the highest good of all of us. It proved true.

The image of God as the unification of male and female is found in Genesis 1:27. It reads:

> *And God created man in His own image, in the image of God created He him; male and female created He them.*

In this Hebrew translation of the Old Testament, we see that the image of God was both male and female—"male and female created he them." God created a blueprint of the soul that was androgynous. Each soul embodied the masculine and feminine aspects and intelligence of God. What he/she created was not unisex individuals — a man and a woman, but rather God created two individuals who both were a perfect blend of masculine and feminine—essentially androgynous Adam and Eve. Each soul was a perfect reflection of the androgyny of God.

> *The Lord God said, "It is not good that a man be alone; I will make him a comparable helper."*
> —Genesis 2:18.

The mythological imagery of Eve being pulled from Adam's rib may be insightfully interpreted as Adam's having had a link to his soul mate inside of him already, within the marrow of DNA structure, but more accurately, in the template of his Stellar Heart. God created Eve, the archetypal woman, with the same consideration, that she would be forever bonded with her equal or "comparable" complement and remain as his equal in the Garden. The mythological Adam and Eve may be seen as stellar twins complementing each other through their unique stellar harmonies and co-creative design. We might imagine them as having resided within the rapture of their unified consciousness with God until "the Fall" that tossed them out of the Garden. Whatever this original sin was, it divided the soul of man.

Plato discussed the concept of soul mates and the androgynous nature of man in "The Symposium."

> *So ancient is the desire of one another which is*

implanted in us, reuniting our original nature, making one of two, and healing the state of man. Each of us when separated, having one side only… is but the indenture of a man, and he is always looking for his other half.

He further suggested that man's yearnings for his twin represent the nature of love itself.

Divine Principle:
God created beauty, love, creative intelligence, grace and harmony. And God gave us free will to choose love's intelligence or to lose it.

The Creator gave the Stellar Angels and their twin complements free will, the choice to travel and use their creativity as they pleased. In the beginning, groups of souls traveled in fields of harmony creating freely and innocently, enjoying their creations. While stellar souls were created in the image of God, their intelligence was not equal to God's intelligence. Many groups of Stellar Angels separated from God's love and created duality —a mess. They cast themselves into darkness, moving further and further from honoring the Mother/Father that created them. Great battles between Lords of Light and Lords of Darkness were fought, and creations of duality filled a universe. The mythic image of the Tree of Good and Evil, which was set before Adam and Eve as temptation, is a poetic image for this choice we have come to know as "the Fall." The garden itself was only a metaphor for the Kingdom of God within, not a primordial paradise on Earth. In truth, the duality of the fall occurred long before the creation of Earth.

The fall resulted in a separation from the true nature of God, the image of God as unified male and female polarities. This separation represents a corruption of the very fabric of the oversoul and its archetypal imprints of a unified dual nature within an androgynous state. We may refer to the separation as a "split soul," as was so aptly portrayed in the picture that my daughter drew of the sun and moon separated across the page. The split-soul imprint was an overlay on the original template, dividing the polarities and locking humanity into an illusionary separation and fixed reality. Just as the atom was split to create a nuclear explosion, the separation of the male and female aspects of the soul created its own disaster for humanity. It has denied us true equality of the sexes and rendered feminine intuition and wisdom as irrational and useless. A long legacy of suppression of the feminine mysteries emerged because of this split-soul imprint. It is the feminine aspect that, as the intuitive function, receives the revelations of God and sees into the many dimensions of our sphere. Without the all-seeing eye of God in the center of her forehead, one is third-eye-blind and limited to a worldview of a fixed reality.

How did this separation called "split soul" emerge when the oversoul was created perfectly in God's image in the beginning? A clue may be found in Genesis 1:26, which says,

And God said, "Let us make man in our image, after our likeness: and let them have dominion over the fish of the sea, and over the fowl of the air, and over the cattle, and over all the earth, and over every creeping thing that creepeth upon the earth."

God said, "Let us," suggesting that more than one were involved in the creation of the Earth and humans.

The Roman church councils, however, rejected the idea of more than one God, dismissing the biblical use of the plural "us" as merely meaning that God was perhaps communicating with his angels about his creations.

Before monotheism, most cultures of the world honored many Gods and Goddesses who they believed created the universe, the Earth and its inhabitants. A Navajo creation myth tells of the holy ones who hung the stars in the sky and sowed each plant on Earth, only to have a trickster Coyote create chaos and cause the great flood. A Greek creation myth offers a chaos theory, a dark void from which earth and stars and clouds were created. There were innumerable gods. Prometheus, one of the Titans, created people, designed to be superior to the animals his brother had created. He made the people walk upright and stole fire from the god Zeus to give to humans. These many Gods and Goddesses ruled the Earth in much the same way that the patriarchal image of One God has been viewed as overseeing and intervening in human affairs.

The Gnostics, a philosophical movement that included the various mystical initiatory religions that flourished during the first few centuries of the Christian/Common era, held a clear distinction between the highest, unknowable God and the Demiurgic "creator" of the material universe. The Demiurge, which means, "master craftsman," was one who imitated the divine model in creating the cosmos and the material plane. Lacking the Supreme Creator's perfection, he created a flawed universe. Plato, who likely influenced Gnostic thought, refers to the Demiurge in the Socratic dialogue Timaeus as the entity who "fashioned and shaped" the material world. The benevolent Demiurge along with the

Archons, "rulers," as in the planetary rulers (planets and con-stellations), presides over the material realm and, in some cases, presents obstacles to the soul-seeking ascent from it. For Gnostics, the world, owing to the above, is flawed and a prison for its inhabitants, but through "Gnosis," knowledge of its levels, root and mysteries the seeker/initiate can tran-scend it.

The Earth with its evolutionary plan was really a grand experiment created by a council of Stellar Angels who thought they could raise themselves and all the fallen angels back to a place of honor and glory through a plan of redemp-tion. It was their strongest desire to end duality and to return to God's grace. Materialization at the third dimension was created as a physical plane of limitation, a fixed reality, which would be a humble proving ground for learning the lessons of love. Through suffering and limitation, each individual was meant to renew his love for God and God's perfection and to choose love over all else. An evolutionary plan, in which humans would evolve over thousands of years, was drawn up and set in motion. Some of the Stellar Angels seed-ed themselves onto the Earth, taking the form of a third-dimensional archetype, Adamic Man. Implanted with a split soul overlay, they denied themselves a unified intelligence and descended into a limited consciousness. Separated from their higher intelligence, they remained humble lifetime after lifetime, evolving their intelligence and improving them-selves through the lessons they chose.

Other Stellar Angels or Lords of Light, like Archangel Michael and Gabriel, remained in a dimension above overseeing and creating harmonies from their seats in the heavens to stimulate, guide and ensure that this evolu-tionary plan would proceed without interference.

Known as the *Divine Plan*, it included an accelerated period of consciousness-raising in the last years of Earth's evolution that would awaken multitudes of evolved souls to their creative potentials and to their destinies to serve an evolution of consciousness on Earth. Reawakening to the power of the light within their hearts, they would begin a process of cleansing and purification to reintegrate the unified aspects of masculine and feminine intelligence. The evolutionary plan also included a promise to honor God above all. Twin complements were to reunite during the final chapter, as they had many times before over the course of Earth's evolution, to complete the karma they had with each other. They were to realize their divine connection as the unity that God had intended in the beginning and honor their promises to each other. The course was set as a divine destiny for humanity and for the Earth.

A recent period, the "quickening", awakened many to the potentials of their higher intelligence. It opened many hearts to the presence of God in their lives and sparked imagination to envision a more positive future, should enough of humanity grow to the intelligence of love. Through consciousness raising efforts, many awakened individuals teach us that a mass consciousness shift will occur that will eventually transfigure the Earth and its inhabitants, completing Earth's evolution and redeeming humanity in God's eyes. However, the creative legacy of evil has proved more resilient than expected, and as prophesied, there were many false prophets, as well as doomsday plans orchestrated by Dark Lords.

A dream offered through the tender heart of an adolescent girl, reveals a God-driven salvation plan. In the dream, God's image is a unified intelligence, a bright glowing light sitting on a throne that welcomes the dreamer into a brightly lit room in two distinct voices, one male and the other female. The final days are revealed to her as an escalation of the war and a world shadowed by pervasive darkness. As the last scene, God's light appears on Earth, all surrender their arms, fall humble and ascend into God's light.

God's plan, introduced to humanity by Jesus Christ, offered the same kind of promise for salvation in the end. In the Revelations of John, it is viewed as two separate events, the Rapture and the Second Coming, promising salvation through God's grace only after an apocalyptic period. John's vision was of a "second coming" of Jesus Christ who would liberate humanity from evil and welcome all into the Kingdom of God, unveiled as the New Jerusalem. However, Jesus only spoke of one event that he believed would happen within his generation. He prefaced his 'giving notice' statement by mentioning that no one but the Father knew the exact moment.

> *From the fig tree learn its lesson: as soon as its branch becomes tender and puts forth its leaves, you know that summer is near. So also, when you see all these things, you know that he is near, at the very gates. Truly, I say to you, this generation will not pass away till all these things take place. Heaven and earth will pass away, but my words will not pass away. But of that day and hour no one knows, not even the angels of heaven, nor the Son, but the Father only.*
>
> —Matthew 24:32-36

I sincerely believe the miracle of God's plan will happen in our lifetime at which time twin souls will return to a state of grace within an earthly paradise.

So much of what we know to be true and that which we witness as real, our ordinary reality, is an illusion. It is as if we are wearing "3D" glasses that obscure our perception and limit our view. We are fixated on a reality that is only one level of our continuous creative reality, which actually contains many dimensions. We are denied access to other realms until we are humbly ready to spiritually evolve. Our glasses were created to make us humble again. We will wear them until we have forgiven ourselves, cast out our demons and embraced the love of God to spiritually evolve.

The enlightened state of self-realization arrives with a whole set of misconceptions. All that is blissful is not necessarily God. Although enlightened individuals' consciousness has touched a higher intelligence, retrieving universal truths and higher wisdom out of transcendent experiences, until worthy, the seeker is denied the final initiation necessary to manifest spirit in matter (transfiguration and resurrection). Pursuing God is not enough to redeem us and meditation alone will not offer us the keys to the Kingdom of God. One remains duality bound until the milestones of spiritual evolution have been reached and one has proved oneself worthy to receive the profound illumination of the Kingdom within.

I received a couple of dreams today from a spiritually awakened woman in Turkey that represented a futile effort to reconcile the duality in the world, a burden too heavy for anyone to bear alone. The dreams reveal two distinct intelligences at work, masculine and the feminine approaches to the same problem. The first dream was relayed as follows:

> I am sitting in darkness, my legs curled under me sitting like a huge Buddha statue in darkness. I catch in my hands horror-movie characters, one by one, out of the darkness in front of me. I am putting every character I catch into a box. I am very much enjoying

*trapping them in boxes. They don't seem as horrible,
but rather in despair within the boxes I have put them
in. After some time, I had captured enough, thinking
there were few left to scare people. I begin to connect
the boxes to one another and make a huge box (cube).
I am painting every side of the box a different color to
turn it into a kind of quiz toy. The boxes in which I
trapped the horror characters are movable, and form a
really huge box. I am playing with the cube, changing
the position of the boxes. I have left the cube with the
colored sides out, as a solved quiz box.*

Sitting in the darkness of the mind and contemplating the
logic of a world of dark images and archetypes of evil may
bring the Buddha mind to realization that the world of suffering is a cyclic entrapment that makes no sense. The dreamer, as
mythic magician, is attempting to reconcile a world of dark
images by trapping them in boxes and creating a Rubik's Cube
to solve the puzzle for the world. The image of Buddha, as a
world redeemer, may be an archetype of suffering and entrapment itself, as the mind cannot achieve through logic, in any of
the dimensions of human consciousness, what the heart wishes to achieve. Buddha himself meditated for six years and in
the final days went to the Bohdi tree with the intention of ending world suffering. Although he emerged enlightened and
achieved some degree of consciousness that propelled him to
begin teaching a path of compassion and mindfulness, he
could no more transfigure the world and end the suffering of
others than the dreamer could. The dreamer may have partial-
ly solved the puzzle for herself, but not for the world.

The next dream, from the same dreamer, offers images to
delight in and a more feminine approach to understanding
and coping with the legacy of duality.

I am in a turquoise emptiness. Within it are story-book and fantasy characters that surround me. Like Peter Pan, Tinkerbell, Snoopy, Casper, Snow White, Sinbad, Ali Baba, Sheherezad, Aladdin, the boy and girl in the story "The Red Skates" and many more I can't count. It is very joyful watching them all flying around, up and down. I hear music, but I don't know the melody. I am wondering if it can be Beethoven 40, which was very famous when I was in my early teens. I think it is not Beethoven. It must be Mozart. I want it to be Mozart. Just as I decide to change the music to Mozart, the flying characters join hands and begin flying in synchrony to the music. I forget about changing music or doing anything else and instead watch them in amazement. They are sparkling, shining dust in the turquoise emptiness.

This dream illuminates a dimension of the collective unconscious from which mythic archetypes, as cartoon characters from familiar fairytales, delight the dreamer with memories of the magical experiences of childhood. Unraveled, each character plays a role in an underlying mythology that depicts psychological challenges as conflicts of light and dark. Resolving these conflicts by returning to our childhood innocence and to a more feminine approach seems to be the key to stepping out of the castle of the mind and into the heart where the melodies, harmonies and images of a creative intelligence spring forth from a turquoise sea. A sea of light like the prima material of the cosmic sea from which all life emerges, it is a creative field of endless possibilities. The turquoise, in contrast with the darkness, denotes illumination and movement from the mind to the heart. In contrast with the first dream, the dreamer merely surrenders

to the fluidity of a harmony of creativity rather than to logically try to solve the puzzle. The dreamer, who thinks the
music may be Beethoven and wishes to change it to Mozart,
is distracted from changing the music and altering the harmony that was brilliantly orchestrated by a higher intelligence. As we may remember the two composers, Mozart and
Beethoven, both went deaf in their late years, a fact punctuating the dreamer's genius while at the same time mentioning
her perceptual limitations. She is content now to surrender to
what is being created. There is no need for the mind to
manipulate either the mythic elements or the music, because
the higher self orchestrates its own creative and meaningful
dream, a " happily-ever-after" resolution to all conflict. The
characters joining hands and circling in gaiety reflect this
meaningful evolution in consciousness.

The two dreams offer us a glimpse of the workings of an
unconscious that is split trying to end duality but unable to
unify its own intelligence. The masculine mind is trying to
confine the horror characters and to solve the problem logically, reflective of the masculine approach. The more feminine approach allows for a natural evolution to be generat-
ed out of a turquoise sea of higher vibration, a more passive
receptive approach. Neither is unified with the other nor
able to resolve the legacy for humanity. Try as we may to
creatively solve the duality of the world, it is futile in any of
the human dimensions. Perhaps it is not as important to
grasp the world as to hold it.

The archetypes of the masculine and feminine emerge
from the subconscious as important twin characters in
dreams and myths as well as prophetic visions, such as those
found in the Bible. The king and queen, the prince and
princess, and the bride and bridegroom are the masculine
and feminine aspects at different maturational levels. They

are often depicted on the throne of Glory, at the ball or at the altar in the creative legacy of the mythic imagination, our fairy tales and myths. These archetypes reflect the sovereign honorable aspects of the soul, who complement each other and who are both meant to be brought into consciousness and realized for the balance they depict. In their highest and most innocent expression they are twin lovers, an integrated spiritual force of creative energy with limitless potentials. But in most instances, they are shadowed by shame, like Adam and Eve, and as a result we are denied the fruits of the garden—love's manifesting potentials.

At the dimension of spirit, the male and female aspects are perfect, but at the dimensions of the human soul they are corrupted and negated by suppression of their qualities. Their fall from grace is an archetypal dilemma of our dualistic consciousness, perpetuated by unconscious forces that rob us of the beauty of an integrated soul — the soul that was androgynous in the beginning. We can rise, however, by embracing the image of spiritual unity between sacred bride and bridegroom, consciously entering our hearts to touch their magnificence. Both feminine and masculine aspects, as two distinct intelligences, need to be acknowledged for their individual brilliance, cleansed with light and embraced as goodness and godliness. Our intuition and wisdom must be awakened to rise and become equal to our rational intelligence for the sacred marriage to occur.

One of the few biblical references to the sacred bride and bridegroom, the masculine and feminine aspects, is found in Revelation 18, describing John's prophecy of the fall of the great city of Babylon. In John's vision an angel warns:

> *The light of a lamp will never shine in you again.*
> *The voice of bridegroom and bride*

will never be heard in you again.
Your merchants were the world's great men.
By your magic spell all the nations were led astray.
—Revelations 18:23

"The light of the lamp will never shine in you again" obviously refers to the extinguishing of God's light within the hearts of those who have consciously chosen greed, ignorance and hatred over wisdom and love. "The voice of the bride and bridegroom that will never be heard in you again" represents a loss of power, consciousness and opportunity for the sacred inner marriage between masculine and feminine intelligence, spiritual unity. Because one chooses a Godless existence, one is rendered deaf to the voice of the bride and bridegroom within, denied the whispers of God that come through the heart. Worthiness and redemption appear to be necessary keys in attaining spiritual unity.

Our maleness and femaleness have many reflections in the world, there to be seen in those kindred spirits who have been assembled for our wholeness, resembling the very essence of who we are inside. Instead of appreciating them for the reflection, we often ignore, discount or reject their qualities, the very ones we've needed to embrace and integrate into our personalities to mature. We may deem them so opposite as to label them "aggravating," lacking appreciation for how they coax out our more hidden strengths and talents and how much they contribute to our psychological and spiritual growth. We tend to sleep through the important movie scenes with them, failing to notice their starring roles and to learn from their characterizations. In truth, many of our friends serve as light-bearers into the dark recesses of the unconscious, shining light on our masculine or feminine brilliance. Fate positions these complements on the stage of life to serve our higher consciousness and to help us draw out our masculine and feminine traits into greater definition and balance.

The one who was placed in our hearts first is the complement who resembles us most in terms of our higher unified intelligence. Our Divine Complement is our perfect match, always was and still is. Their qualities are the very qualities we need to integrate to achieve wholeness. It is one of the important tasks of each soul's evolution to embody the qualities, talents and strengths of its twin. This integration involves the soul, spirit and personality and is accomplished only through a lengthy learning process.

Every soul on Earth—knowingly or unknowingly—is on a quest to fulfill the Stellar Promise, to return to a state of grace with their Divine Complement. We are here to embrace them again and make up for times we denied them our love and failed to recognize the love they had offered us. Our beloved's full-circle return as our mate is a co-creative miracle, which points us back to our original promise: to play together in the harmony of God creatively and in constant loving communion. The Stellar Promise meant that we would always harmonize love in communion with our Divine Complements in every dimension and at every destination. By loving them in each incarnation, we would honor God's creative miracle that planted us together. Through the earthly bonds of a conscious relationship, we could touch God's grace and understand God's power.

Divine Principle:
The Stellar Heart is lit by God's light. Within its deepest chamber, the sacred marriage between twin souls is well-established.

By entering the chasm of the Stellar Heart through meditation, we can begin to experience the love that God created in the beginning. The light embodied within the Stellar Heart is a passionate flame of creative harmony, an eternal fire of passionate love that God lit within us. God's light and unified intelligence have been carried within our Stellar Heart matrix for eons, veiled only because of the overlay imprint of separation—the split soul.

The design of the Stellar Heart consists of seven crystalline rays that form an intricate three-dimensional seven-pointed star. Within the chasm of this stellar structure is a matrix coded in a language of light that establishes the authentic qualities of the individual stellar soul and connects it with God. This matrix unifies opposite and complementary polarities: light and dark, yin and yang, and heaven and earth, represented by the inner bride and bridegroom in the bridal chamber. Also set within the bridal chamber, are the unified creative harmonies of twin souls or "stellar twins," who represent still another bride and bridegroom belonging to the most sacred covenant, the Stellar Promise. They reside within the sixth dimension of our individual consciousness, beyond the veil of our conscious minds.

To enter the Stellar Heart and to move beyond the seal that separates us from the bridal chamber is to gain firsthand experience of our internal unity and androgyny, as well as the promise of God's first creative miracle, eternal unity with our twin soul. Upon entry, we are infused with the light of God and our authentic self is revealed and realized in the light of renewed consciousness. We are bathed in light and anointed by the light, our ego dismembered, our soul purified and transformed, and our consciousness lifted into the deepest chamber. There we commune with God through reunification with two sacred trinities, two signatures within a matrix that initiate us into their mysteries. First is the trinity signature of the male and female polarities unified with God to create a powerful creative intelligence that is balanced, integrated and purposeful. The unification signature code within the bridal chamber is symbolized as X, the merging together of heaven, V, and earth, Λ, male and female. Second is the trinity signature of stellar twins, spiritual soul mates, infused with God's love, expanding, harmonizing and magnifying God's power through their communion. They bridge their light intelligence at dimensions beyond our view through this link in our hearts. The stellar twin signature code, symbolized as > <, two rotated V's merging toward unity, draw the two harmonies of twin souls together. Reawakening to our union with God through these two distinct trinities has been humanity's unconscious striving ever since the fall that separated us.

Although few have envisioned the intricacy of the matrix of the Stellar Heart, there are familiar trinity motifs (symbolic images), some archaic and others out of medieval history that point to the mystery of the encoded signatures within the bridal chamber.

Triskele

The oldest trinity symbol of interest appears on what is considered to be a tombstone or monument in Newgrange,

Ireland and dates back before Stonehenge at about 3200 B.C. This petroglyph consists of three conjoined clockwise spirals forming a mysterious trinity design. Christian monks in the ornate illustrations of the Book of Kell used a Celtic symbol called a triskele, a slight variation of this same symbol. It is thought that these early Christian monks used the triskele to symbolize the Holy Trinity, inserting it amongst other images and calligraphy on the elaborate calfskin pages that they painstakingly copied from the original texts of the gospels.

Celtic interwoven symbols like the "triskele" are said to hold the key to the great mystery of life and are a part of a spiritual legacy of pagan societies. A variety of modern interpretations have been attributed to triskele. The most popular belief is that it represents eternity. Those more familiar with Celtic mythology however, believe it likely represented the cycle of birth, life, and death, or perhaps the three aspects of the triple goddess, the maiden, mother and crone, worshiped from about 500 BCE by pagan cults. We do not know for sure what esoteric meaning the Druids attributed to this symbol and why it was so prevalently used.

The spiral itself is an archaic central symbol often considered both solar and lunar. Its winding spiral moving toward the center can be interpreted as the soul's journey to its core, toward God and the God-self. The symbol emerges from deep within the collective unconscious as part of a symbolic legacy pointing to our original connection to the Source. The trinity design of the triskele incorporating three spirals, in my opinion, represents the earliest symbol depicting our tri-unity with God within the bridal chamber of the Stellar Heart. Whether or not Celtic societies understood the mystery of unification is a question that remains unanswered. However, the trinity design clearly was a sacred spiritual symbol used thousands of years before Christianity's Holy Trinity motif.

Sacred Heart of Jesus

Another familiar image, the sacred twin flames depicted in the iconography of the *Sacred Heart of Christ* can be seen as a likeness of the eternal aspect of complementary harmonies rising above the human heart and beyond the human condition. This iconographic representation associated with images of Jesus, for some, expresses the risen Christ who unifies heaven and earth, light and dark, male and female. The image offers us a glimpse at twin flames, "stellar twins," lit by a passionate fire of stellar light, a fiery light that emerges deep from within the bridal chamber. Christianity interprets the iconography of The Sacred Heart as the passionate fire in the heart of one who is in spiritual service to humanity. However, more likely, the two flames, like wings of the dove, point to the spiritual dimensions of twin-soul communion. Merging twin flames as spiritual harmony, ignite the heart to reflect a passionate creative energy.

A more descriptive image of the *Sacred Heart of Christ*, verifying the "twin soul" meaning, was revealed through a synchronistic experience. I walked into a coffee shop and was greeted by a young girl wearing a tee shirt with The *Sacred Heart of Christ* printed on the front. Instead of the usual depiction, this artist's rendition was of two "blue birds of happiness" hovering above the flaming heart each carrying a banner in their beak. One banner read, "sweethearts," and the one beside it read "straehteews". The backwards spelling of "sweethearts, of course, meant, "opposites unite!"

Star of David

The Star of David, the six-pointed star also known as the Seal of Solomon, is another important divine symbol that has been coded within the collective memory of humanity. It represents the unification of opposites, the internal sacred marriage between masculine and feminine polarities. The symbol is formed through the unification of two triangles, the triangle with one point at the top and the inverted triangle pointing down. They merge to unite spirit and matter, heaven and earth. The triangle pointing up represents the masculine polarity. Fire is its element. The feminine, inverted triangle, whose element is water, rises to merge with the descending masculine fire to create the balance of fire and water at the heart of the initiate. This unified symbol is emblematic of the living Christ, one who is reborn to his or her divine state of perfection as a Son or Daughter of God. It is imprinted within each individual, holding its creative potentials of a unified consciousness dormant until the initiate is awakened to his or her spiritual destiny.

Fleur-de-lis

Yet another mystical symbol and motif of great importance is the fleur-de-lis. The symbol, with its three-foil pattern, is considered to be a stylized Yellow Flag iris or a lily. King Clovis of France adopted it in the 7th century as the insignia of his sovereignty and reign, and his successors continued to use it as a coat of arms. According to legend, Clovis adopted the fleur-de-lis as a coat of arms after receiving a vision from an angel who told him to discard the three crescent moons that were his previous insignia and replace them with the fleur-de-lis.

The fleur-de-lis emerges as an important symbol in every culture throughout time. Its roots can be traced back to Mesopotamia in the third millennium B.C., where it emerges as a mystical symbol imprinted on cylinders. It also has been found imprinted on necklaces, scepters and other artifacts from ancient Egypt, Crete and India, perhaps denoting royalty. In Gnostic Christianity, it is associated with the cult of Mary Magdalene and was considered emblematic of the vine or bloodline created by her union with Jesus Christ.

With its three-foil pattern, the fleur-de-lis represents a significant spiritual trinity whose meaning has been deeply embedded in the collective soul of humanity. I discovered its truer meaning after a member of one of my dream groups shared a dream about the closing chapter of her relationship with her Divine Complement.

In the dream, the dreamer was in a car with her ex-husband, her soul mate. They stopped at a house she described as old and dilapidated. He asked her to go into the house and retrieve some of his personal items that had been left behind. When she entered the house she saw it to be empty. However, on the tiled floor of the bathroom were three items: a pair of purple tinted sunglasses, her husband's wedding ring and her Girl Scout pin. She picked them up, returned to the car and presented them to her ex-husband. The symbol of the Girl Scout pin was most intriguing, because it is similar in design to the three-foil fleur-de-lis, symbolizing the spiritual trinity of synergy at their hearts. Coupled with the wedding ring it grew in significance to require further interpretation. The Girl Scout pin and the wedding ring had been left behind so that the dreamer might come to respect that the covenant of her marriage had represented a sacred promise, much like the pledge of a Girl Scout, one of faithfulness. Although the house of their marriage had been emptied, the Stellar Promise, as a pledge of eternal commitment, would be preserved beyond the reality of the failed relationship. They continued to be linked at the heart and in the psychic field of the dream dimensions.

Although some authors have suggested that the fleur-de-lis is a phallic symbol, while others assign it a feminine connotation, because of its association with the cults of Mary Magdalene, its trinity motif suggests a tri-unity of consciousness. I offer that its spiritual meaning is representational of the divine union between Divine Complements, man and woman unified with God sharing their root in the House of

God, the Stellar Heart. In this vein, the symbol's association with Mary Magdalene is emblematic of her divine relationship with Jesus Christ, the trinity created out of their union with God. The fleur-de-lis may continue to be regarded as a sacred symbol, but one that points us to our hearts to appreciate the sacredness of twin soul communion and our eternal unity with God.

Archetypes and symbols spontaneously emerge out of the collective unconscious as dream images or visions and are often the subject of visionary art. Artists, who deliver meaningful material to the mainstream as logos designs and other symbols, are frequently inspired by the dimensions of spirit. Through their art they deliver meaningful clues conveying higher truths from un-seeable dimensions. Even within pop culture and counterculture, we find interesting examples of symbolic spiritual material in art.

Not long ago, I experienced a great deal of synchronicity with two separate logo designs on the tee shirts of passersby. Everywhere I went they were staring me in the face, day after day. The Volcom™ logo and Roxy™ logo, familiar surf wear company insignias, were of interest to me because they portrayed a trinity motif that I immediately recognized as symbolic for the Stellar Heart and its encoded elements. The stylized artistic renderings of the matrix of the Stellar Heart portrayed in each of theses logos offers evidence as proof of an unconscious memory that exists within us all, a memory that touches deeply the twin trinity signatures within the bridal chamber. Whether or not either of the artists who conceptualized these logos knew the significance of what they were drawing is inconsequential. It is evident, however, that each artist portrayed the elements of the Stellar Heart symbolically with accurate detail.

Volcom™ Logo

The Volcom stylized quartz stone has an angular fleur-de-lis pattern at its center. Its crystalline trinity geometry is simply sketched and stylized forming a striking as well as meaningful logo design. Besides representing its company, it stands as a representational schematic of the Stellar Heart, portraying opposites: dark and light, yin and yang, male and female. The angular trinity at the center, creating the facets of the stone and resembling a fleur-de-lis pattern, remarks on the sacred trinity uniting twin souls within the bridal chamber. Volcom boasts that its company was birthed out of a counterculture's radical response to America's values, a seemingly unlikely place for such a meaningful symbol to have emerged.

Roxy™ Logo

The Roxy™ logo is rendered as two halves of a heart within a larger heart, and yet within another heart. It forms a trinity motif with the outer heart as "the one," the center white heart as "two" and the two pieces of a split heart combine together to form "the three." Within the interior halves are two merging pieces or imprints, > <, that I immediately recognized as the signature code within the bridal chamber that unites twin souls. This code can be accessed through a deep heart-centered meditation or can emerge as a lucid image in a dream to those awakening to its mystery. What is most remarkable about the Roxy logo is that it so poignantly depicts the division, "split soul", as a split heart.

The Volcom and Roxy logos are symbolic evidence of the deepest memory in our hearts, a signature and imprinted code that unifies opposites, male and female, and links twin souls to God within the bridal chamber. Along with tee shirts that have the word "MATRIX" printed across the chest, these two logos point us directly to our hearts so that we might awaken to the inner mystery of the bridal chamber.

The inner marriage, transforming our consciousness back to the original state of unity, is our spiritual aim at this time in evolution, a fact punctuated by the images of logo designs we encounter on occasion. These logos are symbolic elements of an unfolding dream helping humanity recognize the heart center as the entry into God's Kingdom. Through our encounters with these symbols, we are constantly reminded that the Kingdom of God is never too far away. It is centered at our hearts and at same time interfaces our world. These logos stimulate unconscious memory and awaken our minds to the more hidden dimensions where we are "one with" God and in sync with our twin complement.

The mystery of the bridal chamber has remained veiled from our consciousness hidden in the dimensions of our spirit.

However, there is evidence that the mystery of the sacred marriage between sacred bride and bridegroom within the bridal chamber was taught by Jesus to his disciples and disseminated through Gnostic writers for about a century after the crucifixion. Several references to the bridal chamber can be found in what are considered Gnostic gospels contained in the Nag Hammadi Library, as well as one reference in the Song of Solomon of the Old Testament. Passages in both the Gospels of Philip and the Gospel of Thomas, loosely describe the bridal chamber to be part of an initiatory experience or sacrament that unites the bride and bridegroom, ending the separation from God and culminating in the birth of the Christ within.

In the Gospel of Thomas, Jesus made mention of the bridal chamber as the place where he was united with God. From the following passage, it appears certain that he considered the bridal chamber the inner sanctum of his own heart, where he was spiritually fulfilled and glorified.

> *They said to Jesus, "Come, let us pray today and let us fast." Jesus said, "What is the sin that I have committed, or wherein have I been defeated? But when the bridegroom leaves the bridal chamber, then let them fast and pray."*
>
> —Thomas 27.

Through his teachings, Jesus illuminated for his disciples that there was no separation between he and God, as he defined himself as unified with God within the bridal chamber. It is clear that the bridal chamber Jesus refers to is an interior chamber where he is "one with" the Godhead and from which he will not be separated. Not a temple or a church, but the inner temple of his Stellar Heart. Through it, he is "awakened divinity," having emerged reborn as the Son of God—

Christ. Therefore, no spiritual preparation such as fasting and praying were necessary to prove his worthiness or devotion to the Godhead. In his heart and mind, he was God manifest. Only if he as the bridegroom were to leave the chamber of unification, failing in some way, would he need to humble and redeem himself again. Through this passage, Jesus points the way for his disciples and for all of us, toward a unity of consciousness with God through the sacred marriage.

The Gospel of Phillip further illuminates the nature of the bridal chamber. Although some of the Coptic text in the following passage was damaged or corrupted, the meaning remains.

> *The holies of the holies were revealed, and the bridal chamber invited us in....Those who are separated will unite...and will be filled. Every one who will enter the bridal chamber will kindle the light, for...just as in the marriages, which are...happen at night. That fire...only at night and is put out. But the mysteries of that marriage are perfected rather in the day and the light. Neither that day nor its light ever sets. If anyone becomes a son of the bridal chamber, he will receive the light.*
>
> —Phillip 84:23-85:20.

This passage describes a profound initiatory experience, a rekindling of the light within. "The separated will unite," suggests that through entry into the bridal chamber, one is initiated and resides in the light of consciousness of the mysteries of the sacred marriage. It is through the eternally lit fire, a chrism, and light of God that one is purified and anointed to rise as a Son or Daughter of God. He or she receives the light and remains in the light and becomes unified with the light through the experiences within this brightly lit chamber. It is the unification of the bride and bridegroom that gives birth to the Divine, the Son of the bridal chamber—the Christ within.

The Gospel of Thomas and the Gospel of Phillip, the only remnants of the mysterious initiations of the bridal chamber, were only rediscovered in 1945 in Egypt's Nag Hammadi Library, which houses fourth-century papyrus manuscripts. They were excluded from the New Testament perhaps because they were not understood entirely or because they contradicted the material of the other Gospels and threatened the Church patriarchy's newly formed religion. Much of the intended meaning of the passages is difficult to decipher and has been subject to a variety of misinterpretations. Even amongst scholars of Gnostic Christianity, the most common interpretations consider the bridal chamber to refer to a portion—if not the whole—of a ritual initiation that was outwardly performed rather than inwardly achieved. Some scholars believe the ritual of the bridal chamber represented the five stages of initiation performed within Solomon's Temple: baptism, chrism (anointing), Eucharist, redemption and resurrection. However, passages in the Gospels of Phillip make it clear that the water of the baptism and the fire of the chrism were really experiences of the interior bridal chamber. The anointing was not with hot oil but with and of the light.

> *It is because of the chrism that Christ has his name...he who has been anointed possesses everything...the resurrection, the light, the cross, the Holy Spirit. The Father gave him this in the mystery of the bridal—chamber.*
>
> —Philip 53:10-25.

The name "Christ" means the "anointed one." It's the anointing experience within the interior bridal chamber that appears to give rise to the Christ within. What is illuminated through this passage is that the initiation of the bridal chamber accomplishes the resurrection. The cross, likely, takes on the pre-Christian symbolic meaning of "spirit in matter" and the Holy Spirit—the meeting with the Divine.

Phillip likens the bridal chamber to the "Holy of Holies" of Solomon's Temple in an earlier passage. This analogy suggests that the mysteries of the bridal chamber were known and likely part of an outward initiation rite and ritual conducted at the Temple during Solomon's reign. We know that Solomon, who succeeded his father King David as King of Israel in 971 BCE, built his elaborate Temple of Solomon as a Tabernacle to God basing its structure on keys of esoteric wisdom, cosmology and philosophic principles. The domes, arches, pillars and carvings, many gilded in gold, all held symbolic meaning pointing to mystical secrets of initiation used for spiritual illumination. There were three main areas of initiation at the center of the temple: the Ulam, the porch of the structure described as a Cosmic Temple, the Hekal (Holy Place), and the Debir (Holy of Holies). They are viewed as three separate symbolic temples of transfiguration through which the initiate would have been spiritually transformed and awakened to the God-self. The Cosmic or Universal Temple, representing the universal harmony of all creation, was decorated with the Archons, the constellations and planetary rulers that influence a man's psyche and from which he must resurrect his divine light. The second arena of initiation, the Holy Place, was symbolically represented as the human body, the material level and the human form as a temple for universal spirit. Through its initiation man is purified, transformed and symbolically resurrected—reborn to his divine nature and spiritual power. The center most chamber, the "Holy of Holies," was considered the dwelling place of God and the Everlasting House. A 20 ft. cubic room lined in gold and inlaid with jewels, it metaphorically represented the heart. It contained three veils, the last leading to the bridal chamber where at the center the Ark of the Covenant was situated. Interestingly enough, the beautiful figures of the cherubim woven into the veil were images of angelic beings of the highest order, appearing as winged lions and bulls. Depicted also as male and female, they were given the characteristics of both men and animals, representing the unification of man's primal nature with the divine. The images of the cherubim, therefore, tie sexuality with spirituality. The high priest would pass through the veil and enter the Holy of Holies once a year, on the Day of Atonement, to offer blood on the mercy seat for his sins. Solomon also engraved the walls of the Temple with likenesses of the male and female principles in celebration of a mystery, one that joined masculine and feminine in unity. Within the chambers of initiation the mysteries of the sacred marriage were likely advanced, perhaps through ritual enactment of hieros gamos. Solomon's Seal, also known as the Star of David, represents further evidence of Solomon's mystical knowledge as a divine magician and priestly King. Emblematic for the unity at the heart, it unifies heaven on earth, male and female.

Orthodox Christianity, whose doctrines and imagery of a patriarchal Godhead forced us into spiritual submission, has asked us to deny the power of God within, making no mention of the mystery of the bridal chamber and the inner marriage—the true path that Jesus lit. The doctrine of Holy Trinity held by Christianity, that of the Father, Son and Holy Spirit, acknowledges only the masculine aspect of God, denying the feminine any place on God's throne.

Within the chasm and the bridal chamber of the Stellar Heart resides the true identity of God, interwoven within two deeply imprinted trinities. Our individual Stellar Heart is our temple of God where the inner marriage and the sacred marriage are consummated. It can be touched through heart-centered meditation, but its potential is only realized through a deeper initiation when one is ready to be spiritually reborn. This heart sanctum holds within it the keys to the gates of God's Kingdom—the promise of "the everything" of God.

To awaken to the internal unity centered in the bridal chamber we begin by consciously entering our hearts. A meditative journey into the Stellar Heart initiates the process that summons us to the love and unity that is housed within. As Divine Complements, we must dwell within our own Stellar Hearts, the bridal chamber, long enough to witness the light that joins us and to realize the power that this union has to spiritually transform our consciousness. In the consciousness of this light, the unified harmonies lending radiance, brilliance and intelligence to each other, are perfectly matched and complementary. Our communion creates the power of God and God-like potentials—creativity abounds and is shared between us.

One of my students had a dream in 1999 that illustrates the unity between twin souls in the bridal chamber, a unity having great healing potentials. While in the dream state, the female dreamer became conscious of her beloved's emotional tension. Their connection and communion within her dream was expressed as her trying to take his conflicted energy out of his body by scooping it up and carrying it into a structure that she defined as an interesting old house. She drew a picture of the house, whose architectural symmetry sparked my insights and recognition of its true representation. It resembled the sacred geometry of the matrix within the Stellar Heart. Her subconscious had constructed an image of her Stellar Heart and rendered it into a metaphoric image of a house whose architecture defined the matrix. The roof had three triangular window dormers, which were positioned as two small dormers on each side of a larger dormer at the center. Set within each dormer was a triangular window. A door to the house remained open, revealing golden light within. I immediately recognized the configuration of the dormers as representational of the sacred geometry within the deepest crystalline chamber of the Stellar Heart, the bridal chamber. As we remember, this trinity signature links twin souls with the power of God, an imprint of their unified consciousness. The triangular shape of each of the windows set inside each dormer reflected the other sacred trinity, male and female polarities harmonized with God. The roof's construction as a trinity within a trinity represented the complete matrix above and behind the chasm of her heart. Therefore, the entire house was her Stellar Heart. It was a house lit by God into which she was pouring her beloved's discordant energy. By doing so, she was unconsciously attempting to heal him of his suffering, sending discord through her heart to be harmonized by God's love.

The crystalline chamber of the Stellar Heart is our internal and eternal home. As the center of our consciousness, its intelligence is linked to the Creator. The trinity signatures inside are remnants of our stellar legacy, signifying our root, a unified intelligence and connecting link to our twin soul. The bridal chamber is a dwelling place shared by two who since the beginning of time have remained in constant communion with each other. Through respect and recognition of the link between Divine Complements, we are offered the opportunity to acknowledge the miracle of God's Stellar

Promise to us that we would share an eternity of experiences with a comparable partner at every dimension. The love we share with our twin soul represents an eternal promise and commitment to preserve God's original creative miracle. The promise was set in stone in the beginning. Nothing, including death, can part the harmony of the two created together by God.

Jesus commented on the bond between a man and a woman by restating Genesis and elaborating on its significance with the following Scripture:

> *"From the beginning of creation, 'God made them male and female.' 'For this reason a man shall leave his father and mother and be joined to his wife, and the two shall become one flesh.' So they are no longer two but one flesh. What therefore God has joined together, let not man put asunder."*
>
> —Mark 10: 6-9.

Within this Scripture is the essence of the Stellar Promise. "From the beginning of Creation, God made them male and female" should be interpreted to mean that God created them, the souls of his children, androgynous, but in their outward expression, only one sex or the other.

"Two shall become one flesh" intimates that because God's first creations, Stellar Twins, were literally once bonded, it is through marriage that this bond is replicated, consummated and preserved on Earth. For this original state of unity to be realized, a man renounces his singular identity to embrace his wife in recognition of the Stellar Promise. The emphasis that Jesus put on the state of oneness, I am sure, was intended to remind his followers that their separate identities must give way to the unity within their hearts. "Asunder" means, "to separate into pieces." Therefore, no man should try to divide two who God had joined together.

Our unity with God is something most of us have contemplated at one time or another. Many have attempted to achieve reunion with God through a variety of spiritual practices, some of which promise peak experiences of transcendence. To seek the pentacle of God may not be as fruitful as to honor God by rekindling our love for our Divine Complement. Our twin is meant to bring us to the epiphany; our sacred union is the closest expression to God's love that we can experience while on earth.

How is it that we did not know about the Stellar Promise? It seems that we were denied this knowledge until we might become innocent and humble again. How, why and when the separation occurred is not as important as how we might now reunite with our twin, conscious of the earlier commitment. Through divine consciousness we can achieve experiences of love that echo the dimensions of God, unifying our hearts to create the harmony of God and achieving expanded states of love that pierce the veil of separation. In this way, we begin to understand God's dimensions and measure.

The union of twin souls within the template of each oversoul cannot be scientifically examined, but it can be known, as we saw with the previous dream of the house of light. Each soul is cognoscente of the tune of their beloved and the melody of their co-created song, at unconscious levels.

Divine Principle:

A conscious open heart recognizes the beloved with certainty, even when the mind is thinking otherwise.

Subconscious intelligence often reveals its proof through dreams that are meant to shine the light on a soul mate's identity. I chatted with a young woman from Alabama recently who shared a significant dream that she'd had the night before. In her dream, she had a tattoo of the comic character Snoopy on her right upper arm. She thought that was odd until we examined whom Snoopy represented. She said she associated the character with a man she had dated over a five-year period. Their romantic relationship cooled off after two years, primarily because he resented that she had had numerous lovers before she met him. He seemed unable to let go of his judgments about her history. They called it quits and have remained good friends. The dream revealed the permanent imprint on her masculine side, suggesting that the man she knows as Snoopy is the soul mate who complements her masculine power. Like the signature in her heart, the tattoo signifies the permanence of their soul bond.

Most everyone's heart needs opening and healing to break through the defended territory that is often over-guarded. The layers of grief and fear that encase and overshadow the Stellar Promise can deny us our beloved's entry. To help explain, I will use as an example the dream of a woman who was longing for the right partner to enter her life.

In the dream, the dreamer was tending a garden that seemed abandoned. She dug into the ground and found a hole where dirt caved in as she dug. When she dug deeper, she ran into a solid wall of brick. The garden was a metaphor for her heart, which had been abandoned, leaving her feeling empty and with even greater barriers to the love inside, symbolized by the brick wall. The dream then brought her to another garden, where she found some beautiful yellow tulips. When she pulled up a flower, it proved to be joined with a second bulb. She was delighted that she would be able to propagate more in her garden then she'd expected. The tulips symbolized "two lips," the promise of romantic love. Beneath the earth was the unity of twin souls bonded at the root. She had unearthed the Stellar Promise and was shown the work that lay ahead to clear and heal her heart for the reunion. The real healing probably would not come until she had reunited with her Divine Complement. The relationship itself—the intimacy they would share and the healing power of her soul mate's complementary harmony—would help her break down the walls of her heart eventually.

To appreciate the Stellar Promise we need to first recognize that the commitment to love our Divine Complement has divine origins. Realizing that God intended for us to be joined at the hip, so to speak, with another may be an awakening for some but for others a challenge, especially when the design seems to have fallen apart in this lifetime. On the earthly plane, many can't imagine staying married beyond the first argument, let alone making an eternal commitment to love, honor and cherish someone who is an opposite. Whether or not the relationship will endure the hardships that are usually a part of the marriage experience is determined by a willingness to grow and to love one another, weathering the storms, while at the same time not neglecting oneself for the sake of loving someone else. It is not necessary to remain in a bad marriage, thinking God wants us to. Whether the relationship succeeds or fails, the Stellar Promise as an everlasting commitment, will remain intact sealed within our Stellar Hearts forever.

The quest for fulfillment through our Divine Complement relationship is a soul's quest to touch the divine by entering a realm of devoted love. That devotion is for some natural, while others fail and compromise it. To admit that there is one soul mate for us is much like honoring that there is one God.

We put our faith in one who loves and honors us, and we set him or her above all others. The quest for the beloved in this life is similar to the quest for God. What we are seeking seems evasive, not of this world, and beyond the ordinary and magical. It will bring us to our knees in the humblest surrender.

Chapter 3

The Sacred Bride and Bridegroom:
Jesus and Mary Magdalene's Legacy

Divine Principle:

Every savior or redeemer of the world had a Divine Complement.

> *While the King sitteth at his table, my spikenard*
> *sendeth forth the smell thereof. A bundle of myrrh is*
> *my well-beloved unto me; he shall lie all night*
> *betwixt my breasts.*
> —Song of Songs, 12, 13.

*T*he bride and bridegroom, as sacred lovers, reflect the sacred spiritual connection between Divine Complements. Nowhere do we find a more beautiful example of the sacredness of divine lovemaking and devotion between two souls than in the Song of Songs, also known as the Song of Solomon, in the Old Testament. The poetic dialogue of yearnings and praises between the bride and her bridegroom deliver the reader into respect for the spiritual nature of romantic love and the spiritual bonds between two lovers, bride and bridegroom. The Song is thought to be associated with the ancient rite hieros gamos, a sacred sexual ritual with anointing and erotic lovemaking that was said to transform and uplift the lovers to their God and Goddess nature. Within their bridal chamber, the bridal lovers were given the opportunity to transcend their humanness to touch the Divine and to unite in celebration of each other's divinity. This rite offered a transcendent path that was tied deeply to human sexuality and to the spiritual bonds that linked sacred lovers.

Despite the fact that Orthodox Christianity did everything in its power to deny humanity the recognition of Jesus' Divine Complement, and to deny his sexuality, from the immaculate conception to a portrayal of Jesus as a monastic and celibate Son of God, it takes only a little research to find strong evidence that Jesus had embraced a sacred bride. The unification path of enlightenment would have led him to the reflection of the Divine Feminine in someone linked to his masculine soul and embodied in a woman who would have helped him to fulfill his destiny, as he would have helped to fulfill hers.

According to the Gospel of Philip, "There were three who always walked with the Lord; Mary, his mother, and his sister and Magdalene, the one who was his companion. His sister, his mother and his companion were each a Mary."

With the synchronicity of the name Mary in Jesus' life, we see an unfolding of a divine destiny pointing the initiate, Jesus, toward the many faces of the feminine aspect of God— the Triple Goddess (mother, maiden and bride). His destiny before him, Jesus was nurtured and matured through the relationship with his mother, the reflection of the mother principle. He was offered a reflection of feminine innocence through his sister, the maiden, and brought to love by his consort, Mary Magdalene, his sacred bride. Mary, his mother, and his sister Mary we might imagine were early feminine expressions who would help him to psychologically mature and shine the light upon one more Mary. She is the Mary who would become his companion, a disciple he would love more than all the other disciples, and a twin complement sister-bride he would cherish as friend, wife, and lover.

Like all heroes before and after him, Jesus' quest for enlightenment brought him into direct relationship and communion with the Goddess archetype of his subconscious, reflected in the one whose destiny it was to shine the light into his soul. Her mythological representations reveal her as Queen of the Heavens and Earth and as the Goddess of Love, Aphrodite. Her human reflection was the one who expressed these inborn qualities of love and passion best, Mary Magdalene. By descending to her wisdom and earthy nature, as well as ascending to her throne to honor her, he was liberated from his masculine ego and initiated into a mystery, one linked to the bridal chamber of his heart. Touching and embracing her divinity and wisdom, he would have been reborn to his own divinity. Through her heart, he would have been moved into direct communion with God, enlightened to love, and reborn as the Christ King.

The fragrances of the feminine followed Jesus throughout his days and played significant roles in his life, a creative play

that would help him to appreciate the feminine soul, the intuitive and nurturing aspect. The key female characters on the
stage of Jesus' life reflected the mythological archetype of a
Goddess who would enlighten him to the Holy Spirit, the
feminine face of God, and the feminine side of his own
androgynous soul. Women were the light-bearers, reflecting a
divine nature that was complementary to his masculine
strength. He was to learn valuable lessons from each of them
about the power of compassion, nurturing and love. And
through the intimacy of sexual communion with his Divine
Complement, he would come to know the true harmony and
creative force of God.

The name Mary has been given an array of meanings,
about 70 in fact, by scholars who have researched its origins.
In Hebrew, the name is derived from Miriam and Mara, a
name that may have roots in Egypt. The earliest mention of
the name in the Old Testament is Miryam, the sister of Moses
and Aaron, whose name was derived from the Egyptian
Mery (Meryt meaning "cherished" or "beloved"). Although
modern rabbinical definitions suggest Mary to mean "bitter,"
"rebellious" or "sorrowful," an earlier symbolic meaning was
"star of the sea", "drop of the sea" or "myrrh of the sea."

The titles "Star of the Sea" and "Myrrh of the Sea" reflect
images of the primordial figure Aphrodite, the Greek
Goddess of Love, birthed out of the ocean. She is the feminine
archetype of beauty, passion and love. As the Goddess of
love, painted by Renaissance artists who brought her to life as
a naked beauty standing on the platform of a shell, she
reflects the sacred feminine emerging complete, brought into
consciousness. She is likened to the spiritual force of sacred
sexuality that transforms shame into passion and liberates
our creative and loving nature. However, Aphrodite also had
a reputation as an adulteress and temptress who had

untamed passions, sought consorts for divine lovemaking and bore children out of wedlock. She sparked jealousy among the other Goddesses. Mortals, demigods and gods alike fell to her sexual enticements shamelessly. The shadow cast on her divinity is much like the one cast on Eve, who after having partaken of the fruits of carnal knowledge fell into shame and disgrace. The same shadow of shame was cast upon Mary Magdalene, portrayed as a harlot, whose destiny it was to help reconcile the image of the fallen Eve.

The title, "Star of the Sea", given to Aphrodite, is also shared with Isis the Egyptian Goddess, who is also known as the Queen of the Heavens. The mythology surrounding her offers an example of a resurrection myth, in which she combs all of Egypt to retrieve the scattered pieces of her dismembered husband. She finds them all except the phallus, which she fashions from a tree stump and passionately brings him back to life to perform hieros gamos, the sexual communion of the sacred marriage. Through this miraculous sexual act, she is seeded with Horus, the divine child and offspring of the resurrected King.

Throughout the Middle East, Aphrodite's representations flourished, depicting her as the Great Goddess from whom all of life springs forth. From the stories from Sumer come the legends of Inanna and Dumuzi. In the south of Sumer, Dumuzi is characterized as the priest lover who gives energy to the grain. In the north, he is the shepherd king who attains God-like powers through his union with Inanna, Queen of Heaven and Earth. (She is also the Canaanite Goddess Astarte, with her consort Baal and the Mesopotamian Goddess Ishtar, sister and lover to the shepherd Tammuz.)

Who was Mary of Bethany, the one who anointed Jesus with the precious spikenard at Lazarus' table? She was the same Mary, the Magdalene named first among those who witnessed the Crucifixion, and the first to see the resurrected Jesus at the sepulcher on Easter morning. She was the companion who, it was said, he loved more than the other disciples (Philip 63:33-64:9). She was his Divine Complement, his stellar twin, whose destiny it was to embody the divine aspect of feminine consciousness, the Goddess Aphrodite, and to anoint her beloved the priestly King. And she would have brought him to her body at night in the most sacred way, as a sacred lover.

Although there is no biblical mention that she was his wife, many have been drawn to the obvious conclusion that Jesus and Mary Magdalene were married. It was against the customs of Judea at the time for a man not to be married, especially if he was to be considered a rabbi, as Jesus is inferred to have been. Therefore, it is most likely that Jesus was married and that his parents, Mary and Joseph, would have arranged his marriage, as was customary. The wedding feast at Cana mentioned in the Gospels, which Jesus attended, may have been Jesus' own wedding feast celebrating his betrothal to Mary Magdalene.

Margaret Starbird, author of *The Woman With the Alabaster Jar*, concludes that Mary of Bethany and Mary Magdalene, who are mentioned in the Gospels 14 times, are one and the same. Mary of Bethany's ritual anointing of Jesus as the priestly King at Lazarus's table would have solidified his claim as the Messiah, as well as spiritually prepared him for the sacred marriage. The practice of dumping the jar of perfumed oil of spikenard was part of the hieros gamos ritual, which would have prepared the King to enter into sacred communion with the Goddess. Early Jews may have revived the ritual based on a similar ritual performed in Canaan and Sumer, where sacred prostitutes, who were considered noblewomen, performed the rites. The dumping of the oil on his head was symbolic of the blessing of the phallus. Mary's wiping the excess fragrance with her long hair at Lazarus' table was a gesture that connected her deeply and intimately with him. It is not likely that anyone less than his spiritual spouse and one who was a high priestess of the temple would ritually anoint him in such a fashion.

Normally, the bridegroom's entrance into the bridal chamber would follow the anointing ritual. "Bridal chamber", in this case, referred to an exterior environment, a sacred bedroom rather than the interior bridal chamber within the Stellar Heart. Completing the ritual, the sacred sexual act was performed, representing the meeting of the human with the divine aspect of the feminine, an act that would spiritually transform the initiate.

Defined, the term hieros gamos is used to identify a divine lovemaking ritual between two divinities, one male and one female, between two human beings (under certain special conditions), or between a human being and a God or Goddess. The ritual would enact the reunification of the split soul of masculine and feminine, giving rise to the resurrected priestly King.

In ancient Mesopotamia, it was enacted as a ritualized public sexual union between the king and a hierodule ("sacred prostitute"). Human partners became divine by virtue of their participation in the ritual. It was thought, for example, that the priestess who took part in this ritual embodied the goddess Inanna, the Queen of the Heavens. The hieros gamos ritual ensured the wellbeing of the king, the prosperity of the people and the continued fertility of the land.

The only remnant of the rite, which the Orthodox Church included in the Old Testament, is in the Song of Songs. The Church included it despite its suggestive sexual language, believing that it was more accurately interpreted as a metaphor for Christ's love for his church. However, the poem, or "song", was obviously written as a chant between two lovers devoted to each other and in intimate partnership and therefore, could be better applied to Jesus' divine partnership with Mary Magdalene. Although many consider the Song of Songs to have been written to Solomon as a poetic narrative of hieros gamos, a tribute to the King, some have associated the poem with Mary Magdalene because of the verses remarking on a woman's dark face and garments, akin to the Black Madonna, whom Mary Magdalene was said to have embodied. For whomever the Song was written, it holds universal value as the song between any two sacred lovers consummating their love in a spiritual communion to touch the divine spirit of God within themselves.

Jesus and Mary Magdalene were Divine Complements, twin souls, linked to each other's hearts through the bridal chamber. Having both incarnated to be together, fulfilling the Stellar Promise, their individual destinies led them to a mutual one. Theirs was a profound spiritual mission, one meant to offer humanity the keys to the Kingdom of God within, to point all communities toward their hearts in compassion for others, and to offer themselves as divine human examples of God and Goddess, Sacred Bride and Bridegroom. Mary must have been at least an equal in that she was his stellar complement, whose destiny it was to be afforded as much esteem and whose similar legacy might serve to punctuate his.

There is evidence that Mary was a highly esteemed noblewoman of means directly related to the Hasmoneans, who were an order of priests descended from the House of Aaron, the first high priest of Israel. According to Laurence Gardner, genealogist, historian and author of *The Bloodline of the Holy Grail*, there is a likelihood that a dynastic marriage between Jesus and Mary Magdalene occurred, as it would have united and forged a tighter bond between the kingly line of Judah and her priestly royal line of Aaron. With an aristocratic and wealthy lineage, Mary may have helped to support Jesus and his ministry.

The fact that Mary had anointing privilege indicated her priestly and spiritual function in the community. As a high priestess of the temple, she would have been the holder of sacred knowledge. A high priestess's noble duties included anointing and blessing of the spirit of a departing soul so that it may progress to the heavenly realm, as well as performing the initiation rites of the sacred marriage.

The sparse and less-than-complimentary description of Mary Magdalene in the four Gospels offers few details about who she was or as to her relationship to Jesus. The only identifying references are that she was the one from who seven demons were cast out (Luke 8:2 and Mark 16:9). This description has led most to the conclusion that Mary Magdalene was a sinful woman whom Jesus had saved from evil possession. In Christianity, the casting out of demons was translated literally, suggesting that she was possessed by demonic forces and therefore mad before the exorcism. Because of this description, Mary has been stigmatized, scorned and painted as a prostitute and a harlot, much in the same way that Eve has been degraded in interpretations of Genesis as the temptress who cast herself and Adam out of the Garden by eating the fruit of the Tree of Good and Evil.

However, nowhere in the Gospels does it say that Mary Magdalene was a prostitute. In fact, she is usually mentioned as first among a group of women who were Jesus' followers. In the Gospel of Mary, a Gnostic text, she is the one disciple sharing her wisdom and Jesus' privileged teachings with the other disciples.

Those who witnessed the Crucifixion were those closest to Jesus, mostly women who brought him their respect and gave relief through their nurturing spirit and fearless presence. At the Crucifixion, Jesus is with those who were most devoted to him, who stood by his side. Again, three Marys are mentioned. The one mentioned first is Mary Magdalene. Besides John, where were the other disciples? The inescapable truth is that they had denied, betrayed and abandoned him, just as Jesus had predicted they would during the Last Supper.

> *Then Jesus told them, "This very night you will all fall away on account of me, for it is written: 'I will strike the shepherd, and the sheep of the flock will be scattered.' But after I have risen, I will go ahead of you into Galilee. Peter replied, 'Even if all fall away on account of you, I never will.' 'I tell you the truth,' Jesus answered, 'this very night, before the rooster crows, you will disown me three times."*
> ——Matthew 26: 31-35.

As Matthew goes on to chronicle, even Peter, who remained in the courtyard at Jesus' inquisition, denied him as Jesus had predicted. Whether or not God had forsaken Jesus was not as obvious as the fact that "man" had forsaken him. The lesson for Jesus in the design of his destiny pointed him back to the Goddess who bore him, his mother, and to the one who loved and complemented him most, Mary Magdalene. He was to honor womanhood and the women in his life for their faithfulness and love.

The betrayal by those closest and those chosen as his disciples must have brought Jesus to a terrible conclusion. He had chosen the wrong people to call his spiritual brethren, his brothers and spiritual leaders whom he depended on to take the sacred covenant to the people of Israel and form the new Church.

Who was it that Jesus revealed himself to in his tomb? It was Mary Magdalene, who had gone to anoint his body and found the stone of his tomb pushed away.

> *Then Joseph brought a linen cloth, and taking down the body of Jesus, he wrapped it in the cloth, and laid it in a tomb...When the Sabbath was over, Mary Magdalene, and Mary the mother of James, and Salome bought spices, so that they might go and anoint him*
>
> —Mark 15:46, 16:1.

Jesus stood before Mary Magdalene and asked if she did not recognize him. She was the first to witness the resurrection, the miracle transfiguration of Jesus into his God self. And she was to run to tell the other disciples of the miracle that he had risen. She was the first because she was his wife and the one most intimately connected to him.

Divine Principle:
The myths of the resurrected King and the Goddess as divine consort are deeply imprinted remnants of a divine plan to return us to our God/Goddess nature.

Following synchronicities, like the number of Marys in Jesus' life, as well as deciphering meaningful clues and etymology, such as the root and meaning of the name Mary, reveal an unfolding mythic journey and destiny plan to Jesus and Mary Magdalene's lives. We begin to witness the interconnectivity

between antiquities' myths and a history that expressed archetypal themes, the undercurrents beneath their lives events.
There was a mythic dimension to their lives as there is to all of
existence.

The life, death and resurrection of Jesus can be compared
to several resurrection myths that are part of the collective
legacy of earlier generations. The most fascinating similarity
to Jesus' story is the myth of the birth, death and resurrection
of Adonis, the Hellenic Greek God whose consort was none
other than Aphrodite, the Goddess of Love, and Mary
Magdalene's namesake. Adonis is also known as Tammuz in
the myths of Syria and was still worshipped by some Jewish
sects at the time of Christ.

The Adonis myth dating back to 150 to 300 CE, prophesied
the birth of the Son of Man, who would later offer humanity
the method of redemption and an example of a fully manifest
God, adding to the prophecy of Isaiah.

By drawing parallels between biblical narratives and the
myth of Adonis and Aphrodite, one notices that Jesus' story
follows the same mythological theme (birth, death, resurrection and reconciliation between God and Goddess). It also
possesses a great number of the same symbolic elements, ones
I will highlight later on. These parallels reveal that the Adonis
and Aphrodite myth was truly Jesus and Mary Magdalene's
underlying mythology. As twin complements, they were born
into the world with their destiny map in hand, or rather a
myth imprinted in their souls' intelligence, one that had been
transmitted to the consciousness of humanity centuries before
and preserved in oral tradition. The myth represented a master plan for spiritual evolution reuniting the God and Goddess
to reconcile the separation—split soul—and to unite twin
complements to serve a mutual mission. A crucified celibate
Godman who resurrects as a sacrificing savior was not the

master plan for humanities redemption nor was it the authentic story. The mythological plot included the reunification of God and Goddess as integral to the plan for reconciliation of the fall.

The Adonis and Aphrodite myth illuminated Jesus and Mary's journey as twin complements toward self-realizing milestones, enlightening them so that they might fulfill their God-driven mission together, a ministry of great importance and one that was meant to afford Mary as much dignity and recognition as a spiritual teacher as was given to Jesus. To some degree, the myth cast Jesus and Mary's fate offering many opportunities to choose an abiding love, no matter what the challenge or demand on them, and to learn the lessons they had chosen for their incarnation. Therefore, it predicted the hardships they would have to endure such as the crucifixion and their future exile, the final outcome. It laid out the plan for their destiny together, one that would fulfill the Stellar Promise as well as a powerful spiritual mission to serve humanity by example. We can be certain that they were well aware of the impact of this myth on their lives.

By looking at the elements and events of Jesus' story, we find that Jesus had a great deal in common with Adonis. First, the name Adonis, meaning "Lord," holds similarity to the Semitic word "Adonai", a title that Jesus carried throughout his biblical history. Although there is little to connect the Semitic language to the mythemes of the Greek Adonis, the obvious similarity has led many to the conclusion that it was not a mere accident but the result of a primeval unity in language. In other words, the similarity arose as synchronicity. Second, there is archaeological evidence that the site in Bethlehem where Jesus was born and which had been sanctified as his birthplace for two millennia, was a pre-existing sacred site of worship dedicated to

Adonis. Third, it is said that the blood-red anemones sprang up on the hill on which Jesus was crucified and on the Mount of Beatitude, where Jesus was said to have given his first sermons, just as they sprang from the blood of Adonis after Aphrodite blessed it. Coincidences? Or, perhaps as other authors have suggested, evidence of the mythologizing of Jesus' story by the architects of Christianity. Another explanation offers greater meaning to our existence and to the role that Jesus and Mary Magdalene played in humanity's spiritual evolution. Most of the parallel elements, in fact, represent meaningful synchronicities that emerged out of the mythic dimension and played out in the foreground of Jesus and Mary Magdalene's lives as their destiny unfolded. They remain as important elements pointing us back to a mythic legacy that preceded them, one that still influences consciousness today.

Discovering parallel elements between the narratives of the four gospels (Mark, Luke, Mathew and John) and the resurrection myths of the Hellenistic era, such as the myth of Adonis, several recent authors, including Timothy Freke and Peter Gandy, have concluded that Christian fathers borrowed from the legacy of Adonis as well as other pagan resurrection themes in putting together the New Testament, citing the parallels as proof that Jesus' history (birth, crucifixion, and resurrection) was just another "myth", as in falsehood, with no historical basis. In truth, some of the familiar elements, such the birth date of December 25th were undoubtedly borrowed and used to embellish the narrative story so that it might be accepted and absorbed into the pagan communities whose solstice celebrations of Saturnalia were well established. And other mythic elements like the Virgin birth were literalized to support the notion of Jesus' divine birth and to create an image of Jesus that was less human and more divine, the "Son of God". However, reconstructions and embellishments do not erase a man's existence nor do they diminish the importance of his authentic mythological legacy or his contribution. There was a living breathing Jesus Christ, a spiritual master, who was God's choice to point humanity home to their hearts and to embrace an altogether different image of God, a compassionate loving presence who would want us to love our enemies rather than to wage war against each other. Most of the parallels between Jesus' life and the Adonis myth, in fact, exist not because they were authored in by gospel writers but because they appeared as a string of synchronistic elements within a meaningful unfolding destiny. The course of humanity's evolution was mythically mapped to include the destiny of several world awakeners. One would rise reborn as Christ and alongside his beloved complement would light the way for others. The analogous elements can be viewed as symbolic clues and manifesting signs pointing to Jesus' authentic identity as the resurrected Son of Man and "Lord". The parallels should in fact underscore the importance of Jesus life, rather than to raise doubt as to his existence.

The notion that Jesus' story was a completely crafted and reconstructed myth arises partly out of a failure to understand how myth serves the consciousness of humanity and drives our spiritual evolution forward. Most people do not recognize how prevalent mythic elements are in modern life. For example, The Little Mermaid, the fairytale made into a Disney animated movie, is a modern rendition of the Adonis and Aphrodite myth. Ariel is very much like Aphrodite, birthed out of the sea, a mermaid who seeks to be honored as the authentic bride, an equal to her male counterpart. The fairytale expresses the same archetypal struggle to unite masculine and feminine in the sacred marriage as the 3,000 year old Adonis and Aphrodite myth.

Myths represent our roots, blueprints for humanity's spiritual evolution set into motion eons ago. Myth prophesies our future in the same way that a precognitive dream predicts a day's events. A dream or myth is a hidden archetypal reality that often manifests in the outer world as an interesting and meaningful storyline of events. As public dreams or scripts of the collective unconscious composed of metaphoric imagery like our night dreams, but on a larger scale, myths drive human consciousness forward on an evolutionary trail through deaths, rebirths and battles that act out human psychological and spiritual dilemmas, completing a cycle of humanity's destiny plan, through which all of humanity is to learn the lessons of its fate. With gods and goddesses, demigods and mortal characters as archetypes—powerful energies of light and dark — myths unfold out of unconscious aspects of the collective soul and eventually manifest as real-life dramas that become part of humanity's history. In other words, the hero in the myth of a collective dream is birthed into the world through each individual soul whose destiny it is to act out the part. The hero, as world redeemer, is given the opportunity to fulfill his or her mythic destiny by stepping onto his path consciously and fulfilling each spiritual requirement. In the case of the myth of Adonis, the destiny fulfills a promise of resurrection and spiritual reunification between two separated lovers, bride and bridegroom, to resolve the split within the soul. Myths offer a blueprint or script through which humanity can recognize its evolutionary tasks and evolve for the betterment of the consciousness of all.

As the Adonis and Aphrodite myth unfolds, Adonis was born to Myrrha, a king's daughter whose incestuous romance with her father seeded her with child. Distraught over his daughter's lust for him, the king pursues Myrrha with a sword. Before she could be slain and out of compassion, the gods turned her into a tree, making her invisible.

On the day of Adonis' birth, Aphrodite happened upon the three daughters of fate, Clotho, the spinner, Lachesis, drawer of lots, and Atroposat, who cuts the thread marking the end of life. Aphrodite was shown two threads of Adonis' destiny and was asked whether they should leave a thread unbound. Upon seeing his destiny, the alarmed Aphrodite sped off in her chariot to avert the infant's death. Just as Adonis was about to burst out of the wooden womb, a wild boar, which some say was really Ares in disguise, penetrated the womb of the tree with its tusks. He was just about to kill the infant when the Goddess Aphrodite arrived. She snatched Adonis out of the wooden womb and flew off, carrying him at her bosom. She later entrusted him to Persephone, the dark goddess of death in the underworld, thinking that she may be able to save him from his fate by giving him to the goddess of death herself.

The noble and handsome Adonis later became Aphrodite's lover and mate. As Aphrodite wandered the forest beside him, she sought to ensure that he would not become the hunted. As she called her dogs, she would seek gentle prey, always careful to avoid those creatures to which nature had given weapons of their own, and she urged Adonis to do likewise.

He didn't heed her warnings, however, and sought wilder and richer game for his fire. He caught an ancient wild boar in his lair and pierced it with his lance but could not kill it. It turned on him and pierced his side. Aphrodite responded to Adonis' moans, circling back to find him dead, blood pouring out of his wound. Determined that the memorials of her grief would endure and that neither his life nor his death would be forgotten, she sprinkled the nectar of the gods on his blood. As each drop struck the dust, it became a blood-red anemone.

As a destiny map of two divinely born lovers, one questing to preserve their love and the other seeking personal glory only to meet death instead, the myth to this point follows the archetypal plot of the lovers separated by fate. As the myth proceeds, the resurrection of Adonis and his reunification with Aphrodite is achieved only after great sacrifice and self-determination. By examining the characters of Adonis and Aphrodite as well as interpreting the mythological elements, plot and themes and applying them Jesus' story, we notice parallels that are meaningful and that shed light on some of the hidden details of Jesus' birth and destiny. We unearth information about Jesus and Mary's personalities and the psychological challenges that they probably faced on their personal quest for wholeness, enlightenment and committed partnership.

First, Adonis is birthed out of the tree of Myrrha, symbolically born out of the shadow of an incest wound hidden in the sacred tree of life. The tree, as the feminine in nature, whose bountiful gifts of healing and creative force of power are shadowed by shame and denial, hosted the seed of the noble Adonis. Myrrha's father, attempting to annihilate his daughter, represents the shame cast on a womanhood as well as suppression of her mysteries, wisdom and sexuality. It further comments on the wounding of Aphrodite, Goddess of Love, whose sexuality is at the center of her authentic personality and purpose.

Relating this mythic scene to Jesus' birth, the tree represented his own mother's womb. What was the shadow of shame cast on the soul of Mary, the mother of Jesus and transferred as a legacy to her son? Beyond the obvious legacy of collective shame cast on human sexuality, especially on womanhood, there is biblical evidence that Mary's conception of Jesus was not an immaculate one after all. Various scholars and genealogists have concluded that the marriage of Mary and Joseph was a dynastic one. Despite the fact that the Roman Catholic Church declared that God seeded Mary with Jesus through immaculate conception, the Gospels also insist that Jesus was the authentic Messiah, a direct descendant from the House of Judah through the seed of Joseph. Such contradictions and other discrepancies are encountered frequently in comparing the gospels of Mark, Luke, John, and Matthew. Questions arise, for instance, about whose lines Matthew and Luke are referring to, despite the fact that they both name Joseph as a patrilineal descendant of David. The Catholic Orthodox Church has concluded that Luke is offering the vine or line of Mary, contending that Heli was Mary's father. Out of a quagmire of conflicting theories, one theory follows the mythological hints of a symbolic incest wound. Lord Alfred Hervey, in *The Geneologies of Our Lord*, concludes that Mary's father was Jacob and Joseph's father was Heli and that one line represents the royal kingly line, the other the natural line to Abraham, a descendant of Adam. His theory also suggests that Mary and Joseph were first cousins. We might conclude that this would amount to an incest wound born out of a marriage whose purpose was to maintain the purity of the bloodline of the House of Judah.

Although one might argue that the practice of intermarrying was widely accepted and in accordance with the rules of dynastic inheritance at the time, our soul's intelligence, operating with a different set of rules, appreciates more clearly defined boundaries for sexual intimacy. Any sexual practice that moves against the integrity and innocence of the soul can produce a wound.

Another shadow cast on the birth of the authentic Messiah

is the possibility that his birth was not authorized under the rules of dynastic wedlock. Laurence Gardner has suggested that the birth of Jesus did not coincide with the rules, which clearly spelled out the circumstances in which a King could be born. Jesus was born at the wrong time of the year, (March). According to the rules, a woman could conceive only in the month of December to ensure that the birth coincided with the atonement month, September.

Whatever the nature of the wound, it was cast upon the feminine and passed onto Jesus' soul as a legacy of shame from which out of necessity he would have to be liberated. At the same time, Adonis' emerging from the wooden womb of a myrrh tree represented a "divine birth" out of the tree of wisdom and primordial perfection.

Psychologically, this conflict between divinity and corrupted sexuality would have been reconciled through a divine partnership with the Goddess of Love. It would make perfect sense that the enlightened Jesus would have been delivered out of the shame of his flesh, a deep collective wound that denied him the intelligence of the feminine side of his spirit, through one whose love was meant to heal him. His beloved Mary Magdalene, as Aphrodite, would have been the rescuer/lover who initiated the healing, accomplished through her sexual and spiritual relationship with him. It is also interesting to note that the castration of Uranus by Cronos, an act of sexual liberation, gave birth to Aphrodite.

Another mythological element, which bears significance, is that of Ares disguised as a wild boar. In Christianity, the boar was a symbol of brutality, greed, anger, gluttony, jealousy, savagery, tyranny, the Antichrist, the beast of Revelation, and the Devil. Its rampages through vineyards and orchards were emblematic of the destruction of Israel by her enemies, both temporal and spiritual. Roman warriors carried the image of the wild boar on their shields, helmets and banners. The boar was considered sacred and associated to the goddess Persephone, as its tusks were crescent-shaped. It was said that the boar was split into two when the year was dissected, the light half as the sacred king and the dark as his rival.

Following the mythology, the wild boar's penetration of the tree's womb is a parallel with Herod the Great, the sacred king's dark rival, who as we remember ordered the massacre of all young male children in the region, a desperate attempt to thwart the fulfillment of the Messiah prophecy. Like Aphrodite, the mother Mary, was offered a glimpse of what would be Jesus' fate if she were not to follow the guidance of Joseph's dream, which instructed him to flee Israel for a time. Herod fails to kill his rival, because the maternal aspect, Mary, flees with her husband to Egypt, in much the same way that Aphrodite rescued Adonis by taking him to her bosom after seeing his fate. We know little of Jesus' childhood, because he was hidden in the underworld of his mother's bosom to protect him during his early years.

Following the thread further, Jesus emerges seemingly out of nowhere and seeks glory as Messiah, the rightful King of Israel, a politically bold move against Herod Antipas (son of Herod the Great), his faction and the Romans in general. Like Adonis, Jesus seeks wilder game for his transformational fire, setting out to change the political and spiritual climate of Israel.

Jesus' spiritual-warrior personality may have been determined by the planets, constellations and aspects of his astrology—his natal chart. The myth of Adonis and Aphrodite holds a key element in prophesying Jesus' birth under the sun sign of Aries. In the mythology, the boar penetrating the womb of the tree is really Ares in disguise, the masculine archetype denoting male strength, focused will and warrior attributes along with a darker war-like side. Metaphorically, when Aries, as the sacred-king aspect of the boar, penetrates the womb of the tree and causes Adonis to burst out, it points to Ares' influence in Jesus' astrology at the time of his birth. As his sun sign, the archetype Ares would have defined and driven Jesus' authentic personality to pursue his birthright relentlessly and rebelliously.

Lawrence Gardner has suggested Jesus was a Pisces, born March 1, 7 BCE, and still others proclaim that he was born in September, fulfilling the rules of dynastic inheritance and validating Jesus as the authentic Messiah. However, after unraveling the myth's prophecy and evaluating the personality of the historical Jesus, finding that his personality matched most of the Aries traits, I have concluded that Jesus was born in late March, 7BCE between the 21st and 28th of the month.

By applying Aphrodite's nature to Mary Magdalene, we might suspect that Mary, after considering her beloved's personality, warned him in much the same way that Aphrodite warns Adonis not to trade his life and happiness for glory. As mystical a figure as Mary Magdalene has been depicted to be by the Gnostics, she certainly would have been able to read his fate at least as well as Jesus himself had at the Last Supper. Also, she would surely have feared the cruelties of Herod Antipas, the son of Herod the Great, who had slaughtered most of the Hasmonaeon priests and their family members to whom Mary Magdalene was directly related. It's not unreasonable to conclude that Herod might have murdered some of Mary's closest family members, including her mother.

As it was foretold — Jesus was crucified and speared in the side by a Roman soldier much like Adonis was pierced by the wild boar. The blood, the symbol of Jesus' suffering, is caught in an earthen chalice and transformed symbolically into the spirit and life force of Christ. This parallels Aphrodite's blessing of Adonis' blood with the nectar of the gods, from which blood red anemones sprang forth as his memorial.

In the Holy Eucharist of the Orthodox Church, the wine (blood) and bread (body) of Christ is used to signify the nourishment of our lives. Through it, many celebrate the life, death, and resurrection of Christ and are thereby able to participate in the mystery of salvation. Conversely, as far back as 50 CE, cults that celebrated the life, death and resurrection of Adonis would, on one day, display images of Aphrodite and Adonis celebrating the marriage of the lovers, and on the next day women attired as mourners bore the image of the dead Adonis to the sea and committed it to the waves. Yet they did not mourn without hope, for they sang that the lost one would come back to resurrect the promise of the divine union. Many have considered these summer celebrations as mere fertility rites ensuring a good harvest. However, the mourning of Adonis appears to have been symbolic of the promise of the reunification of Adonis and Aphrodite as a plan for renewal, much like Christianity's salvation plan. Therefore, as a reconciliation myth, it would possess further spiritual significance.

The resurrection of Adonis was accomplished through Aphrodite's descent into the underworld of Hades and his queen, Persephone. Armed with her sword, Aphrodite aims to avenge her beloved's death and retrieve him from the underworld. She threatens to break down all seven gates of Hades, releasing the dead until their souls outnumber the living. Persephone welcomes the challenge and instructs the ferryman that Aphrodite must relinquish an adornment at each gate as payment for her passage on the river of woes. At the last gate, she relinquishes her sword. Upon confronting

Persephone, Aphrodite is faced with the wrath of her competitor, who curses her with every bit of mortal suffering she can muster. However, as the Goddess of Love, Aphrodite is immortal, and although she suffers, she does not die. To resolve the dispute, Zeus, the Patriarch of Mount Olympus, descends into the underworld and offers a compromise. He decrees that Adonis will spend a third of the year with Aphrodite in the light of the world, a third with Persephone in the underworld, and the other third wherever he chooses. Adonis chooses to reside the last third with his beloved Aphrodite.

According to Matthew, Mary Magdalene did not have to break down all the gates of Hades to enter the tomb where Jesus laid. She arrived prepared with spices and oils to anoint him the morning after Passover and found the stone to the tomb rolled away and no body within the tomb. Whether it was an angel she saw first or Jesus, a moment later her beloved was very much alive before her.

Some authors have offered the premise that Jesus did not die on the cross at Calvary. Both Gardner and Henry Lincoln lay out the scenario that the Crucifixion was planned to create the appearance that Jesus died and was resurrected to fulfill the prophecy of Isaiah. After all, why wouldn't someone who could walk on water and resurrect the dead (as he did with Lazarus) simply climb off the cross or dematerialize it, for that matter?

Most agree that legends from a small village in the South of France called Les Saintes-Marie-de-la-Mer point to Mary Magdalene's arrival along with family members seeking refuge in a community of Jews who had fled Israel earlier. There is evidence that they began a ministry spreading a Gnostic Christian religion throughout Western Europe. Some, including myself, have gone so far as to consider it likely that

Jesus accompanied her on that journey. The legend reveals that a woman with a vessel arrived in a boat with no oars after narrowly escaping death during a storm at sea. Among the others who were with her was an adolescent girl named Sarah who is commemorated today with a statue and a celebration on her feast day, May 24, in the town of Les Saintes-Marie-de-la-Mer. The legend assumes that "Sarah the Egyptian" was a serving girl to the three Marys—Mary Magdalene, Mary Salome and Mary Jacobi—who are celebrated for bringing Christianity to the Roman province known as Gaul. However, Margaret Starbird has concluded that Sarah was Jesus and Mary's first-born child.

As we interpret the mythology of Aphrodite's descent, we understand that it is the power of her love and her sheer determination that resurrect Adonis. For Mary Magdalene, the surrendering of earthly adornments may have taken the form of relinquishing everything in order to flee Israel after the Crucifixion. A legend held by Eastern Orthodoxy says Mary went to Rome after the day of the Pentecost and confronted Tiberius Caesar in protest of the condemnation of Jesus. She announced boldly, "Christ has risen," and took an egg from the table and held it in front of Tiberius as a symbolic gesture. Caesar laughed and said that Christ's rising from the dead was no more likely than that the egg in her hand would turn red. Before he finished speaking, the egg in her hand turned a bright red, and she continued proclaiming the Gospel to the entire imperial house. The red Easter egg has been used since that time in the Easter feast, symbolic of Christ's resurrection.

Like Aphrodite, Mary was armed with a vengeance, delivering a righteous and bold message to Tiberius. He must have taken her message to heart, because he soon removed Pontius Pilate from his position in Jerusalem and transferred him to

Gaul. The red egg, as a fertility symbol, represents rebirth, resurrection and renewal, but perhaps also points to the fertility of the Goddess holding it. Was Mary Magdalene pregnant with Jesus' child? Several authors have concluded that Mary was indeed carrying the child of Jesus, before she fled Israel.

Gardner and Lincoln offer compelling evidence that Mary Magdalene had not just one child, but two, Jesus and Joseph supporting a theory that the bloodline of Christ continued through patrilineal descent, fulfilling the rules of dynastic succession. However, in light of the legend from Les Saintes-Marie de la Mer and supported by my dreams and intuition, I am in agreement with Margaret Starbird's conclusion that Mary's first child was "Sarah the Egyptian," the young child who accompanied Mary, Martha and Joseph of Arimathea. Jesus and Mary's second child was named Josephes. Each child, symbolic of a divine birth and conceived out of the sacred union, would have resurrected the bloodline of Christ and thus perpetuated the seed of David in future generations.

After the Crucifixion, the resurrection of the word and teachings of Christ would have been fulfilled and carried forward through Mary's ministry. She would have directed her attention to teaching, in her own style, the wisdom she had attained through her own spiritual development as well as the teachings Jesus had passed on to her. If Jesus ascended to God and was no longer with her or humanity, her commitment to spread the faith and teachings of Jesus would have been paramount. Based on the legends of her cult in the South of France and the evidence of churches sprinkled throughout western Europe, which Starbird suggests were originally dedicated to her, not to the mother of Jesus as they are now, it is clear that a Gnostic Christianity flourished for quite some time. It ended abruptly with the Albigensian

Crusade in 1209 A.D., which forced the Cathars, a Christian sect that may have held her teachings sacred, into retreat.

The image of the Black Madonna and the Black Sister/Bride depicted by statues scattered throughout Western Europe has been associated with Mary Magdalene and her Gnosis (true wisdom) as well as her darkened and shamed image. The Black Sister-Bride, an archetype of the feminine, represents the darker aspect of the feminine, akin to the image of Persephone, who is the initiator into deeper mysteries of the underworld. To understand the personality and psychological turmoil of Mary Magdalene as the Black Madonna, we must consider her wounded psyche, arising from her underlying mythology as Aphrodite. Mary Magdalene would have embodied both goddess aspects, those of Aphrodite and Persephone. In Greek mythology, Persephone is a virgin maiden separated from her mother, Demeter, the fertility mother goddess. She is betrayed by her father, Zeus, who allows his brother Hades to rape her and pull her into the underworld to become his queen. She is allowed to return to her mother every spring and regains her virgin status once more. She, therefore, represents a goddess of death and rebirth, held captive in the darkness of a legacy of shame surrounding her sexuality until she is renewed in spring, returning to the light of the world and to the side of her mother. Aphrodite, on the other hand, keeps her sexuality sacred and untainted. These two archetypes, which are almost always in opposition, represent powerful forces in women's psyches. They emerge and renew their authentic qualities as women heal themselves of a legacy of shame and wounded sexuality that has been cast on the feminine soul since the fall of Eve. And it is Eve that Mary Magdalene came to punctuate in her era as part of humanity's plan to reconcile the fall.

Mary's own journey to rescue her beloved would have led her first to address the wound of her own feminine soul. Her Persephone personality would have reflected wounds of a defiled and degraded feminine in opposition to the love and liberated sexuality of the Aphrodite archetype in her unconscious. We might imagine that on Mary's journey toward self-realization and wholeness, she would have had to confront shame, neglect and self-ridicule, stemming from her own sexual wound, as well as sorrow surrounding the separation from her mother, who was killed along with other members of her Hasmonean family. Persephone's cursing her with every possible bit of mortal pain, would have likely caused Mary Magdalene to suffer continued degradation. We have only to look at Peter's attitude toward her in the Gospel of Mary and the Gospel of Thomas to conclude that she was seriously disrespected for being a woman. Of Mary, Peter said:

> *"Let Mary leave us, for women are not worthy of life." Jesus responded, "I myself shall lead her in order to make her male, so that she too may become a living spirit resembling you males. For every woman who will make herself male will enter the kingdom of heaven."*
>
> —Gospel of Thomas 114.

What Jesus may have meant with this equality statement was that he would help Mary to develop her own masculine intelligence and strengthen her spirit to become as bold and masculine as he was, and therefore worthy of God's Kingdom.

As Aphrodite confronting her rival Persephone, Mary Magdalene confronts the archetype of death, reflecting a woman's tendency to submit, surrender to fate and remain powerless. She must resurrect her own inner masculine attributes, reflected to her in the qualities of her beloved Jesus and strengthen her will to reclaim a new sense of pride and become as courageous as he. Her journey into the under-world accomplishes the healing of both the inner masculine and the feminine spirit, renewing a balance of intuition and rational intelligence. She would emerge as healer and humanitarian, and Goddess of Love. The underlying Adonis/Aphrodite myth offered her the same opportunity for the resurrection of consciousness, enlightenment and redemption that it did for her beloved Jesus.

It is likely that fate presented many challenges for Mary to conquer in serving her higher mission with Jesus. Her faith and faithfulness would have been tested many times during the course of their ministry. Likely, the most difficult test was at the foot of the cross. Her script's role, as the rescuer of Adonis (Jesus), would have demanded that she do something beyond standing helplessly accepting the death of her god, something contradictory to what we have been told by the nar-ratives of the Passion. She would have done everything under the sun to protect and save him. Just as the myth of Adonis and Aphrodite prophesized Jesus birth and the many other ele-ments of his life that parallel with Adonis, it pointed to a reso-lution that involved the willful action of his beloved Mary, an act of her bravery and one that would ensure the survival of their promises to each other and to humanity. What did she do? I have concluded that she arranged a miracle, orchestrated with the help of others, a timely rescue from cross that allowed them both to flee Judea and travel to Gaul together. This con-clusion fulfills the prophecy of their mythology and supports what other authors like as Lincoln, Baigent, Leigh and Gardner have brilliantly laid out, convincing arguments that Jesus did not die on the cross.

The archetypes of Adonis and Aphrodite drove Jesus and

Mary's creative purpose forward through self-actualizing milestones, which would have brought them closer together, appreciating the reflection that they were to each other. Like all complements, they would have been healers to each other, cleansing the legacy of shame that denied their authentic qualities, the sacred nature of their sexuality, and the balance of the male and female within their individual souls. Each of their paths would have been the path of unification, through which they would have become enlightened and united to serve a greater purpose for humanity.

The way that Jesus lit was the path of unification, because it is the only direct path to Christhood and the path that initiated him. It should be obvious after examining the mythology that Jesus was the embodiment of Adonis, Godman, and that Mary was the embodiment of Aphrodite, Goddess of love. Fulfilling their promises to each other and completing the tasks of their mutual destiny, they were to light the way for all of us, a way that honors complementary partnership and fulfills the Stellar Promise. Jesus undoubtedly realized and fulfilled the Stellar Promise, understanding that he could not resurrect to his God-self without the loving support of his Divine Complement, Mary Magdalene and the other Marys who offered him even more reflections of the feminine face of God. As bridegroom, he reconciled the "split soul" through the sacred marriage and unified his consciousness with God so that he might reside in the kingdom of his heart in complete recognition of his divinity. He had realized Christ consciousness and became God manifest, as it was his destiny to achieve.

Saying 22 of the Gospels of Thomas explains the path that Jesus lit. When Jesus' disciples asked, "Should we enter the Kingdom as children?" He replied:

*When you make the two one, and when you make the
inside like the outside and the outside like the inside,
and the above like the below, and when you make the
male and the female one and the same, so that the
male not be male nor the female ... then you will
enter the kingdom.*

—Thomas 22.

With this statement, Jesus illuminated the path of unification with God as a complete metamorphosis of the soul rec-
onciling the split between masculine and feminine. "The
two" within that are made one merge heaven and earth, spirit manifest into matter. With the realization of the equality
between male and female as the outer reflection of an inner
perfection, one is enlightened and reborn to their spiritual
light, eternal unity with God and perfection. The doors to the
Kingdom are opened. Jesus also taught the necessity of honoring the feminine aspect of God, the Holy Spirit, above all
images of God. Jesus said:

*Whoever blasphemes against the father will be forgiv-
en, and whoever blasphemes against the son will be
forgiven, but whoever blasphemes against the Holy
Spirit will not be forgiven on earth or in heaven.*

—Thomas 44.

From the Gnostic perspective in Christianity and for
Qabbalists, the Holy Spirit represents the feminine aspect of
God, "Mother God," offering new clarity of meaning to the
passage above. It appears obvious that Orthodox Christianity's
reinterpretation of the Holy Spirit to mean the aspect of the
Father that infuses our experience, "intercession," was a slap to
the feminine face of God, denying the feminine spirit any

honor and rendering all women ungodly. This same view denied Jesus' Divine Complement, Mary Magdalene, any importance or place of honor within Christianity, and any role in the redemptive plan.

The mythological blueprint for reuniting the Queen with her King, a most divine union that fulfills the Stellar Promise, appears to remain unfulfilled for the rest of us. Christianity's version of the story, a resurrected Jesus Christ acting on behalf of humanity as savior and world redeemer, has not remedied the cycle of suffering on earth. Undoubtedly, because it did not offer the same path that Jesus lit. As a result, the world is still a wasteland separated from the Goddess of Love. Patriarchal suppression of feminine intelligence and wisdom and a lack of recognition given to the Sacred Bride have denied us a feminine image of God. Without the recognition and veneration of the Sacred Bride, humanity's split soul remains un-reconciled.

Divine Principle:
The Bridal Chamber of the Stellar Heart holds the promise of everlasting life—our immortality.

Revelation 21 reveals the return of the Lamb, Jesus, with his bride. She is dressed in fine linen, and although John appears to have interpreted her as the New Jerusalem being revealed to Jesus, she appears as the image of the Divine Feminine, summoning all to her splendor and to the Kingdom. The Orthodox Church has continued to perpetuate the interpretation that any mention of a sacred bride refers to

Jesus' love for the Church, his bride. However, anyone who has traveled beyond the confines of this interpretation and into the mythic dimensions of the soul's labyrinth or explored the mythologies of the world has been met by the image of a feminine archetype, a goddess, who initiates the journeyer into her mysteries. The reconciliation of the split between her and the true masculine complement culminates in the sacred marriage and wedding feast, representing the fulfilling promise of God's abundant possibilities manifest on earth.

Without the Sacred Bride there can be no inner marriage or resolution of the fall, no nurturing of the heart, or abundant feast to fulfill our dreams. The bride is lost, discarded and abandoned and her image blackened and disrespected. The keys to the kingdom are locked away in her heart and until her wisdom is welcomed we are not redeemed.

A legend pointing to the 'lost bride', as integral to the solution and redemption of the world, is the Quest for the Holy Grail. Seen as a quest for spiritual illumination and immortality, the Grail is revealed only to one who is pure of heart and bold enough to seek its mysteries. In the numerous versions of the legend of King Arthur and the questing hero Parsifal, the King is portrayed as having a mortal wound, symbolic of the suffering of his kingdom. The Grail reflects that which restores king and kingdom to health. Though its power is held in a chalice, cup or other vessel, it is clear there is a feminine holder who presents the chalice at the feast. She is seen as a young woman carrying the Grail in a procession behind a young man who is holding a blood-dripping lance. She passes it among the knights and the King at the table, and all feast on the bounty it brings forth. The young Parsifal, who is bewildered by the power of the Grail, fails to ask the question that will illuminate the Grail's mystery. As a result, the kingdom falls to famine and further plight, and it is not until he finds the Grail Castle again four years later that he gets his second chance to ask, "Whom does the Grail serve?"

Some have interpreted the Grail to be symbolically specific to the chalice Jesus used at the Last Supper and the cup that caught the blood of Christ at the Crucifixion, which Joseph of Arimathea later carried to Gaul. Still others suggest it represents the Sangrael, the blood royal of the direct descendants of Jesus. We should not, however, separate the Grail from the carrier of the Grail, the 'lost bride' and feminine complement, who if remains separated from her king the world would be left a wasteland. Her God-inspired wisdom is served to those who seek her out and welcome her to their hearts. Symbolically, the Grail represents unification with Christ, holding the promise of healing, immortality and fulfillment. The lost bride summons all in the "spirit of Christ" to recognize who it is the Grail serves—the consciousness of all.

The Second Coming, the reunification culminating in the wedding feast, represents humanity's ascension into the Kingdom of God, through which all receive God's salvation. It offers the same hope as that of the Grail quest and of the ceremonies and celebrations of Adonis, which held the promise that when Adonis returns, his reunion with Aphrodite would bring about a restoration of the culture. The imagery of all three mythological motifs points to the return of the resurrected God or King, not as a lone savior of the world, but alongside his feminine complement. Their unification represents the long-awaited Stellar Promise and reconciliation of the fall.

This mythic salvation plan is contained in each of us, hidden deep in the bridal chamber of the Stellar Heart, where the bride and bridegroom have always dwelled in perfect unification with God. As Jesus said, "The Kingdom of God does not come with your careful observation, nor will people say, 'Here it is,' or 'There it is,' because the kingdom of God is within you." (Luke 17:20, 21)

The Kingdom of God within the Stellar Heart holds the promise of everlasting life in communion with God. The legacy of human separation from the Bridal Chamber and the seemingly never-ending evolutionary spiral of duality that resulted from the fall are in their final chapter. Through God's creative push, a miracle reunion of the Christ and Christa, bride and bridegroom, will transfigure our reality, and we will ascend to the Kingdom that God created for us—a world lit by God's light.

Interpretation of the Twin Centered Rose

The anomaly of the twin-centered rose in and of itself can be appreciated for its beauty, rarity and perfection. Its blossoms unfold to form a trinity-matrix design of complex unity and symmetry. The full singular outer blossom houses a mystery in its center: two symmetrical unfolding bud centers unified together to resemble the yin-yang symbol of balance and unity of opposites. The two within the one, a sacred trinity, expresses the unification of opposites within the totality of the One, as well as the unification of twin souls in the bridal chamber of the heart.

Symbolically, the ordinary red rose represents a complex symbol of heavenly perfection and earthly passion. It is often depicted at the center of the crucifix in Christian iconography as an emblem of divine love. Rose gardens evoke the paradisiacal location of the mystical marriage between Adam and Eve. In mythology, the red rose is associated with the passionate beauty of the love Goddess Aphrodite (Venus) and its redness with the blood of Adonis. Interestingly enough, this mythological association of the rose reflects the mystical union of the God and Goddess archetypes and is the underlying mythology of the sacred union between Mary Magdalene and Jesus. Today, red roses are bestowed as gifts of love, appreciation and devotion by lovers everywhere on Valentine's Day. Roses also adorn altars to the Divine Mother.

What the camera lens captured was a divine imprint of meaningful imagery. The imagery within the twin-centered rose encapsulates a story of spiritual evolution between Jesus and Mary Magdalene, as sacred bride and bridegroom. Jesus is depicted beneath what appear to be palm branches, symbolic of Jesus' personal glory, righteousness and victory. Palm leaves were used in several celebrations, one of which is the Feast of the Tabernacle to the glory and triumph of the Israelites. We know that upon entering Jerusalem on Nisan 10, the day for the selection of the Pascal lamb to be sacrificed for the Passover supper and days before the Crucifixion and Resurrection, crowds waved palm branches as Jesus rode into Jerusalem on a donkey. The crowds waving palm leaves celebrated him as the true King of Israel. Some authors, such as Lawrence Gardner, suggest that Jesus deliberately made his entry into Jerusalem on that day to enact the prophecy of Isaiah 53, which would have solidified his claim to the Davidic legacy. It is logical to interpret the pose beneath palm branches in the left bud as a snapshot of Christ's glorified state just before the Resurrection.

Did Jesus, in seeking recognition as the true King of Israel, turn away from his beloved Mary for a time?

The imagery conveys that while Mary was turned toward her beloved, Jesus had turned away from her, perhaps in favor of his personal quest for self-realization and the fulfillment of his individual destiny as the Son of Man. Perhaps he lacked appreciation of Mary's worth to his spiritual unity with God and it wasn't until his transfiguration that he realized her divine connection to him through an initiation in the bridal chamber of his Stellar Heart. The imagery of the spirit form of Christ, emerging from the bud and standing in front of his beloved, remarks on this spiritual transformation that turned him toward his twin complement again in recognition and in love. He appears to be ready to reveal his heart to her and embrace her as his sacred bride. The imagery almost reminds us of the resurrection scene that occurred when Mary arrived at the tomb after the Crucifixion to anoint the body of Jesus. He appeared to her in the sepulcher on Easter morning as an angel, and it wasn't until moments later that he identified himself to her as Jesus.

Looking closely at the right bud, we see that Mary is adorned in head veil and is seated in repose. She humbly faces her beloved as if expecting him to rise to the power of love. The image certainly denotes her divinity in connection to Jesus. Looking closely, we notice that she is embraced by another figure whose arms appear to cradle her. These arms seem to emerge from a larger-than-life feminine deity situated behind Mary in the outer folds of the right bud. This figure might very well represent the feminine aspect of God, the Holy Spirit, supporting Mary's spiritual evolution and healing her from the shame of separation to resurrect her soul to its divinity.

The unfolding story in the photo represents a remarkable spiritual revelation, pointing to the divinity of the relationship between Jesus and Mary Magdalene. As a focal point in the right bud of the rose, Mary reconciles the split between god and goddess, inspiring us to venerate her and bring her out of the shadows of obscurity and perceived irrelevance to Jesus' life. It cannot be denied that what was captured by the camera was meant to be regarded as a divine communication, understood for its intrinsic truth and preserved for its spiritual value in helping us to appreciate the divine union between Mary Magdalene and Jesus Christ after centuries of misconception.

Chapter 4

Fall From Grace

Divine Principle:
The beauty of our Divine Complement is reflected before our heart. It is our heart that calls the beauty forth. And it is the heart that must persuade the mind to shed all the illusions of conditioning.

So much of what the media has fed us about meeting a potential partner is a thick soup of unconsciousness that feeds desire, neglects the heart and poisons the soul. Singles enter the dating arena with many misconceptions about how couples attract, meet, converse, and end up happily married. Many believe that if they have the right formula, look a certain way, say the right line, have the right attitude, they'll snag the perfect man or woman to "love, honor, and cherish."

Reality TV shows such as *The Bachelor* and The *Bachelorette* epitomize the darkness that has fallen on courtship. On *The Bachelor*, women are pitted against one another in a cutthroat competition to win the symbolic rose of devotional love given by someone who appears to be near-perfect, as handsome as handsome can be, and every woman's dream of Mr. Right. He narrows the field each week, rejecting those who displease him or who don't match his ideal. In the end, that one special girl gets the engagement ring, the symbol of a future betrothal, placed on her finger in an oh-so-romantic setting. Whether the couple makes it all the way to a lasting relationship isn't as significant to the audience as who's chosen.

The unconscious drive to be chosen from among others through competition has its roots in Greek mythology. Paris, a handsome demigod, was commissioned to decide once and for all who was the most beautiful and desirable goddess on Mount Olympus. Athena, Hera and Aphrodite were all contestants. Each possessed her own elements of desirability. Athena was known for her intelligence, wisdom and physical strength. Hera was the wife of Zeus, and her throne would mean glory for young Paris should he choose the goddess representing faithfulness and commitment to her husband. Finally, Aphrodite was the goddess who was birthed out as Venus, the goddess of love and sexuality, whose pelvic girdle no man could resist. After each of the goddesses met with him privately, alluring him with their promises, Paris contemplated his choice. Athena offered him valor, Hera honor and position, and Aphrodite sexual fulfillment with a bride equal to her, Helen of Troy. In the end, Aphrodite wins the golden apple. Paris couldn't resist the one with sex appeal. The other goddesses left without reward and, in a fit of jealousy, plotted the destruction of Troy.

This myth represents an enormous unconscious drive that leads even the most sincere man to plummet from grace and into the temptations of lust. Everywhere we look, we are sexually enticed by images of ideals. Beautiful expressions of feminine and masculine archetypes of Aphrodite and Apollo are portrayed on the covers and pages of leading fashion magazines. Our celebrities are glamorously attached to the perfect-looking partners and their romances blown out of proportion until they resemble fairy tales, complete with "happily ever after" endings. The public is enticed and conditioned to seek ideals that are in no way real.

Good-hearted and intelligent men and women are judged on body type, sex appeal and whiteness of teeth. The average individual will view 60 billion images of the perfect body type in a lifetime. From the lines and contours of buxom women to the broad shoulders of muscular men, the body beautiful is set before us every day to be worshipped and admired. Some scientists argue that attraction to specific body types relates more to primitive drives in identifying fertile mates than it does to the stimulus of the cultural archetypes of beauty. Their findings reveal that men tend to idealize an hourglass figure, as it denotes fertility in a woman, and that women will choose a man with angular facial features and broad shoulders as a sexual partner but will choose a mature, nurturing and soft-featured man as a husband because those features are more fatherly. However, there is no correlation between the size of a man's shoulders and his sperm count or the size of a woman's breasts and her reproductive abilities, therefore this theory makes little sense.

With so much pressure to look attractive, singles can fall

into despair if they don't believe they can compete physically. They develop addictions to perfection and neuroses that devalue and degrade them even further. They often abuse themselves for gaining a pound or two or not working out enough. Some may spend thousands of dollars on cosmetic surgery and countless hours at the gym trying to attain the perfect shape.

The desire for perfection and the longing to be seen as beautiful by others, especially by the opposite sex, shadows our self-concept. We may become trapped in a collective imperative of ideals created by the culture, one that denies authentic beauty and compares rather than contrasts. This imperative has little to offer the intelligence of our heart, to which true love and spiritual attraction are more meaningful. It bases everything on physical appeal and sexual desirability, so much so that the spiritual connection is left only to Christian channels on TV or deemed irrelevant altogether.

Mind-sets caused by conditioning railroad our hearts, leading even the most sincere to ignore the beauty of a more spiritually defined connection. The blind mind roams to find an archetype of perfection to adore instead of following the soul's intelligence to the perfect complement. In truth, Divine Complements can attest that it was not their mate's physical appearance or facial features that convinced them that they were the one. It was an intuitive knowing, an understanding of a divine connection and a complementary vibe that convinced them.

Divine Principle:
The blind lover may walk alongside desire content until the path disappears into the light of illumination revealing the one who duplicates God in their heart.

Dating is a pleasurable experience for some and a cruel experience for others. Singles may go to a bar, club or private party and find others like themselves roaming around and mingling, attempting to share a moment in time with someone special. The dating experience can lead to frustration, fear of rejection and even the threat of being stalked. Entering the meat market becomes less and less attractive to those seeking a meaningful relationship.

The dating selection process can offer the most amazing view of flirtatious behaviors, as women vie for attention and men prowl the room. Prowling and hunting is said to be a most natural behavior for men because of primitive biological drives. The same theories say women are likely to wait, wish for and submit to a prowling male. Science has all kinds of observational tools to support its premises on men and women's mating behaviors, as if we were all soulless individuals propelled only by the biological drive to procreate.

A television show called *The Mysteries of Mating* offered scientific evidence that much can be revealed about mating styles by the body language of singles talking during a first date. Behavior such as turning the shoulder inward was interpreted as a positive cue from a woman who is interested in her date. Turning her toes inward—a position called pigeoning—was seen as an act of submitting to a man's interest. It was even suggested that a man look at his date's feet under the table to see whether she's interested. Synchronized movements such as lifting a glass of wine to the lips at the same time were also signs of enjoying each other's company. More negative body-language cues, such as distancing the body, sitting too far apart or with shoulders turned outward and fiddling with one's hair, indicate less interest and attraction. Couples were also put in a poolside-party setting where the scientists predicted who would match based on previous testing of attraction scales. While a couple of their predictions proved accurate, the experiment was less than predictive in most instances.

For those who don't trust their sexual instincts, an interesting gizmo called MatchUp promises to instantly produce a date who's perfectly matched for you. The device is programmed from a computer with answers to a personal inventory of likes and dislikes, personality characteristics, and what one desires in a mate. Answers to questions like, "How many times do you like to have sex in a week?" and "How would you describe your personality, A, B, or C?" yield a list of those whose answers match up with yours. When two devices are linked, they produce raw percentage scores. If the scores are high enough, a couple is on their way to an enjoyable date.

All this should sound like nonsense to those in possession of an intelligent heart, those who will witness their Divine Complements through the lens of their heart and measure their worth not by conditioned drives and cultural imperatives but by divine imperatives. Human-conditioned tastes and behaviors and biological drives are a level separated from soul, spirit and our God /Goddess nature. Though they appear logical to the separated mind, they are spiritually illogical, irrational and meaningless to our higher selves and the heart of the human driven by a spiritual promise.

Divine Principle:
The heavenly web is a creative field where complements co-create the miracle of their first meeting.

With online dating services on the rise, more and more singles choose to surf the Internet to find the ideal partner. It provides a safe route for some and a dangerous route for others. Those who use them say they prefer getting to know someone first via e-mail or by participating in one of the many chat rooms on the Net, rather than roaming bars and nightclubs.

Anyone can match up with someone by submitting a profile introduction. A profile can include a wild array of descriptive anecdotes about one's personality. Everything from "what TV family our family most resembles" to "what substance we prefer to dip our candy bar into, peanut butter or milk." And if we are a descendant of a royal bloodline, we may wish to include a coat of arms. Put up a picture and—voila!—you're ready to be discovered for a date on the heavenly web.

The field can even be narrowed down to those who share our interests. For stargazers, one of the astro-dating services will link you up with someone who has a compatible astrological sign and chart. The sports enthusiast can have a romantic discussion with someone interested in football, baseball or hockey. Vegetarians can eliminate the meat from the "meat market" and find someone who will stir-fry tofu with them. If you are spiritually enlightened, you can try one of the New Age-consciousness sites to begin the quest for your soul mate.

Singles who find it difficult to choose can have an expert narrow the field for them. There is a site that will help anyone discover at last "who they really are" by asking them to complete a 40-minute survey of adjectives that best describe their character and personality. Rate yourself on a scale of "very" to "not at all" on each of a hundred or more descriptions, which include the likes of "lazy," "gregarious," "social," "good-looking" and "intelligent," and you will get a good look at your self-esteem. The site will compile the data and create a 29-dimension compatibility profile that will be matched with suitable possibilities among those surveyed.

The expert on this site mentions that four out of five marriages fail because the wrong mates were chosen. Through a logical, scientific arrangement of an individual's character and constitution, family values, personality, and emotional makeup and skills, anyone can find the right match for a lasting relationship. The site lists few statistics on its success, but we can only guess that it is unlikely that a psychological assessment tool like this one could be more successful at matching someone than is the higher creative intelligence of the human spirit.

A test cannot see into the destiny map of the soul to understand who most serves our higher purpose. Nor can it determine what karmic contracts we have made with one another to balance the scales from previous lifetimes. It does not appreciate the lessons we chose to develop spiritually and that our complement comes into our life to support. Nor can it find a complementary partner who mirrors best our feminine and masculine attributes, bringing balance to our soul. It would not support a spiritual relationship and is likely to send innocents down a path away from their creative destiny and off the edge of a cliff for a great big fall from grace.

Some singles sites post their success stories attesting to love matches that were made on the Web. They can tempt almost anyone to at least think about joining a singles chat. Some Divine Complements do find each other this way, though rarely. They enter the field of "meant to be" and navigate through to the right Internet site through their unified creative harmony. Lo and behold, they lived a block or two away from each other and could have met the next day through some other experience.

A real success story came from a middle-aged woman who said that she tried online dating at the urgings of her mother. As a flight attended, she considered her life satisfying and had resigned to "soulmatelessness' as a second choice. Shortly after her mother died, she created a profile on an online dating site. She received three match possibilities and initiated emails to begin to narrow down the already narrow field. Nothing! Letting go to resignation, weeks later she finally received an email from a man whose responses sparked her heart. Come to find out, he was a customs agent at the very airport she flew out of week after week. She couldn't count the number of times she must have ignored his shining face. To the credit of an online dating service she finally met her Divine Complement, the very man who fate had repeatedly put on her path, but who she had regrettably ignored. Meant to be!

Another success story came from a young man who met his bride through an online dating service. He used the service for about two years and finally found a woman with whom he fell in love. Both were successful doctors with a great deal in common, as both of their families were from India and had migrated to the United States. We might imagine that their families were elated. Whether they are Divine Complements I didn't ascertain, but it sounded like a "happily ever after" perfect dating ending.

Divine Principle:

The divine design of twin souls honors their evolution above the cultural values and traditions of their families. It recognizes God as the ultimate matchmaker.

I wandered into Subway to grab a sandwich for my daughter the other day. Standing behind me in line were a beautiful East Indian couple. Although the young woman was in modern dress, her arms were clad with rows of bangle bracelets, ascending three-quarters of the way up her forearms. Her hands, front and back, were painted with henna in a beautiful floral and heart vine design, a traditional temporary tattoo called Mehindi. She graciously explained that both the bracelets and tattooing are part of the wedding tradition for brides in India. The bracelets are worn for two months as a sign of the bride's recent marriage, and the tattooing is part of an elaborate beautification ritual.

Without hesitation, she said hers was a traditional arranged marriage. She had pledged to her family that she would marry in her Indian tradition despite that fact that she had lived in the United States for many years. She pleaded to finish college before marriage, but once she had graduated, she told her parents she was ready. They asked whether she wanted to meet the groom, a break from the tradition that the bride and groom do not meet until the wedding day. She said "yes," but I sensed she'd had little choice even so. She was comfortable with the traditional values of her centuries-old culture. For her, it would have been impossible to break from tradition and disappoint her family.

Looking through a veil of politeness, I saw an unhappy girl. Her eyes and her hesitation communicated everything when I asked whether she was happy with their choice. She was not. He was not her "match made in heaven," and when I told her that someday she would return to the sacred marriage in her heart, she smiled in agreement and embraced me with loving arms. I was in such shock afterward that I walked out the door without my sandwich, looking for a sign from God. An SUV passed by with a sticker in the window that read "Friction." I knew there had already been friction between two who were undoubtedly mismatched and wondered what course their lives together would take.

Arranged marriages are favored in many parts of the world, where tradition is seldom argued against and it dictates the fate of couples every day, betrothing them for the families' sake rather than the sake of the couple's hearts. A marriage based on practicality and dowry seems unromantic by American standards, where most marry for love and because of attraction. Many who argue in favor of arranged marriages believe that love will follow in due course and that the low divorce statistics prove the marriages are compatible and happy ones. But many others would argue that these divorce statistics prove no such thing, that for many of these couples the stigma of betraying their families is far too great to even consider divorce.

Though it might be concluded that arranged marriages usually deny soul mates their destiny together, it is likely that most soul mates would have considered the legacy of cultural values and tradition of the families they had incarnated to be with very carefully. Therefore, despite how it appears, the destiny design plans and accommodates for these circumstances and soul mates come together through their families' participation in the design. But for some whose evolution demands that they rise to a higher consciousness in ways such as seeking equality in a relationship and exercising free will, great inner conflict is likely to result when the pull of loyalty and the desire for freedom of choice are at odds. And they will fall from grace should they remain loyal to a long legacy of cultural tradition and succumb to family pressures, marrying someone they know was not meant for them.

Divine Principle:
The creative legacy of inequality between the male and female is recapitulated until its shadow on the soul is revealed and denied power.

The unconscious pull toward recapitulating patterns of inequality, male dominance and supremacy continues to be witnessed everywhere, including in the dating selection process. Even in a so-called liberated American culture, where some women have discarded stereotypical roles and impoverished attitudes about themselves and risen to greater equality, we see failure. The rise to equality, for many women, has been achieved by sacrificing their feminine soul and adopting a more male attitude in the world. Rather than swinging toward intuitive feminine power, they are overly dictated by male reason and intelligence. No matter how liberated and self-empowered a woman may appear on the outside, she may secretly wish for a partner who will lead the way and secure the future for her.

Men still seek women who will admire them and submit to their will. Some men find competitiveness in women to be too much to handle and look for more traditional brides who are submissive and can be controlled. They are slaves to an unconscious drive to dominate women's consciousness.

For men looking for inequality in a relationship, there are mail-order-bride sites that offer a bounty of subservient mistresses. These sites and services number over 200 and usually represent women from Korea, Southeast Asia, including the Philippines and Thailand, and Russia and the other countries formerly part of the Soviet Union.

I recently came across a Russian mail-order-bride site that includes an entire page of reasons why Russian women are well-suited for American men. Among the reasons listed: Russian women are more appreciative and unspoiled because they are used to being abused by men in their country; American women are often demanding and hard to please, while Russian women are adoring and appreciative of a man's sensitive qualities; more than half of American women are overweight or obese, while Russian women are rarely overweight, because they are more concerned with their appearance and don't usually have cars and must walk everywhere.

Although we may find this advertisement absurd and obviously degrading to all women, such sites and services are on the rise rather than on the decline.

Mail-order-bride services in America originated in the mid-1800s after many women had been widowed during the Civil War. They were transported West in wagon trains to marry men who had staked their claims and created settlements.

Modern-day mail-order brides are prized not because of shortages of available women but because they are suited for more traditional subservient roles. It appears that the evolution of consciousness has been taking a degrading step backward as many well-educated and mature men insist on subservient women they can mold and control.

The Immigration and Naturalization Service (INS) conducted a study in 1994 in which it surveyed 204 men whose median age was 37 and who had applied for visas for their foreign brides. Ninety-four percent of the men surveyed were white, highly educated (50 percent having two or more years of college, 6 percent with MD's or Ph.D.'s, only five without high school diplomas), politically and ideologically conservative, and generally economically and professionally successful

(64 percent earned more than $20,000 a year, and 42 percent were in professional or managerial positions). The researcher found that these men sought foreign women because they were likely to hold more traditional values—in other words, happy to be a homemaker, asking no more than a husband, a home, and a family. Although the study states that men who choose the mail-order method of mate selection are "above average in their communication skills" and "exceptional in the sense that they are trying cross-cultural marriage to improve their chances for loving and enduring relationships," the researcher cautions that such conclusions are thin at best. His experience and the observations of others show that, contrary to responses in questionnaires, those who have used the mail-order-bride method to find a mate have control in mind more than a loving and enduring relationship.

Asian women who were solicited were in general much younger than the men who responded. Most were impoverished, uneducated women who sought to elevate their socioeconomic status by fleeing their country to marry an American. They idealized American men because they "look like movie stars" and because they found the men in their country less appealing and more cruel and unfaithful.

The gross inequality between men and women that is revealed with such matches often leads to abuse. When a man seeks extreme subservience, he is likely to verbally punish, restrict and even beat his wife to gain more and more control over her. Many of these women are little more than household and sexual slaves who are expected to appreciate their husbands for freeing them from the poverty and repression in their native country. Most of the time, these women find themselves in isolation, separated from their culture and families and unlikely to get intervention or support.

The statistics from mail-order-bride sites on the Internet

and catalogue matching services seldom offer success stories. Few sites post any statistics, and those that do have reported that fewer than 4 percent of the matches they make result in marriage.

Mail-order-bride services are a reflection of the continued inequality between men and women, the degradation of the feminine soul, and the devaluation of women's status. This inequality has permeated cultures all over the world for centuries. Our evolution has progressed somewhat in terms of embracing and supporting equality between the sexes and elevating the status of women to an honorable position, but overall, women fall in status to less status than men, men are elevated to power and both fall from grace in the denial of their equality.

Divine Principle:
The worth and worthiness of another cannot be measured or weighed against the values of the mind. It is redeemed in the heart of the beholder who has witnessed authenticity.

Many singles create a composite picture of the qualities they wish to attract in a mate and set out describing them on a wish list. These wish lists may offer an array of desirable traits and conditions; everything from waist size to how many figures they want to see is their partner's bank account. For some, spiritual orientation and commitment will be important, while others want someone who is easy to please and romantically excellent. At least a couple of people I have known have gone so far as to create a list with more than a hundred attributes and traits.

Wish lists may stand as the ideal for a long time or may be refined again and again after the dating experience reveals the need to add a few qualities that were lacking in the last relationship. Once polished and revised, these lists may look like children's attempts to get everything they want for Christmas. Never considering that the higher self, the Santa Claus of the subconscious, might throw in a few lumps of coal or add a couple of surprises, all for the sake and greater good of personal evolution.

With the expectation set to a height of "perfect for me," a Divine Complement may look disappointing to a wish-list maker because their talents, traits and attributes are complementary, not perfect. Perfection is not achievable on this earthly plane, and the denial of that fact will only lead to disillusion and disappointment. The incessant need for perfection may arise out of a deep need for the perfection of God and God's goodness reflected in a mate. Or it may be the result of cultural conditioning and unconscious beliefs that make our own imperfections irreconcilable.

Wish lists may also arise and be compiled out of deep needs for the things one didn't get in childhood. We may seek what our parents withheld from us, longing to be loved and cared for in order to reconcile the past. Or we may steer away from characteristics we found distasteful in a parent's attitude or demeanor. If, as a child, a man had wanted his mother's undivided attention and felt unheard or even ignored, he may wish for a woman who will never interrupt him while he talks endlessly about himself. He will undoubtedly include in his wish list that she be a good listener, attentive and not interested just in herself. A woman might imagine and desire a man who cooks and cleans. One might suspect she really means she doesn't wish to be taken for granted or put into the role of housemaid. Perhaps her own mother was so wrapped up in cleaning up and feeding her husband that she had no time for herself or to play with her children.

The need for love and friendship will undoubtedly be at the top of most lists. Most people want someone to have fun with, who enjoys the same activities and who will provide true companionship. But wish-list makers sometimes have holes in their hearts they wish to fill with someone else's qualities. They look for things they lack within themselves in a mate, rather than making a commitment to develop those qualities for themselves. They often seek fulfillment in the beginning of a relationship and fail to recognize that love arrives in increments through a couple's achievements together rather than all at once in a happily-ever-after package of positive qualities. Holding unrealistic expectations will usually deny us fulfillment. We may arrive at a banquet table filled with foreign foods and not be able appreciate that all of it will nurture our heart and soul.

Some wish-list makers are likely to create lists because of failed relationships, such as a woman who falls deeply in love with a man because he is sexually attractive and later discovers him to be a womanizer. A woman may vow that she will never again be so irrational as to fall in love with a man in a fit of passion, ignoring his obvious limitations and imperfections. She may have taken an inventory of all the neglect and shortcomings of her last romantic partner and revised her wish list to make it more conservative. Such a woman is likely to feel embarrassed by her ignorance and may lean toward controlling her emotional side more and more. Logic is what she's after, because her emotions and her heart have failed her. Now she believes she must identify the specific qualities she is seeking. A man may do something similar and later realize that his wish list offers him a composite picture of his mother. Many men are so programmed and wired for sex that they are likely to paste Playboy-centerfold images in the margins of their lists.

Those who pursue ideals can hurt their chances of having the most soul fulfilling kind of relationship—one that will evolve them beyond the projections of ideals or anima/animus attraction and put them into the arms of someone they are more meaningfully connected to. Wish lists are deadly to divine consciousness because they never take into account the "meant to be." So that when the Divine Complement is delivered to the door of our heart, it is shut by too many "have-to-haves." Wish-list ideals in no way complement the heart or the potential that two have to grow to love each other through time and through open hearts. Worshipping physical ideals is not a basis for a beautiful relationship. Beautiful people can be wrapped in less-than-perfect packages. A mind that is fixated on a physical ideal or any other ideal will battle the heart for supremacy over and over until it is disarmed by spiritual love and awakened to the power and perfection of God's love. It is through the Divine Complementary relationship that we are most likely to see the face of God and feel God's perfection, not through cuddling up to an archetype of perfection.

A divine state of consciousness will raise us from the fall and grace us with the knowledge of divine destiny between two less-than-perfect individuals matched to make each other feel more divine. It accepts that we get what we need, not what we necessarily want or expect in a complement. Consciousness does not mean that we size a person up based on our wish list but that we appreciate the uniqueness and attributes they bring to us as contributing to our wholeness and our happiness.

Divine Principle:
There is no rushing the creative currents that unite complements. The meeting is divinely timed.

Many search high and low for the right partner. They date for years and are seldom satisfied with the people they meet. Some will keep up the search for their soul mates knowing that they're out there somewhere, while others will be tempted to not wait and end up marrying someone else. The hurdle may be in developing the patience to wait, holding on to the faith that our Divine Complement will arrive at the right time. Our higher intelligence co-creates that divine timing, and all the wishing, hoping and praying won't bring them into our life before we are both ready. Our complement is not likely to be found by prowling or roaming the world in search of them. Although we may be ready for a committed relationship, our complements may not be and they will be hidden in the shadows until they are rebirthed spiritually or emotionally to be with us.

The other day, I walked into the convenience store down the street from my home. A woman was standing at the checkout counter cleaning her sunglasses on the shirt of her male companion. I thought they must have been married forever for her to take such a liberty with him. The young couple said they were on their honeymoon and were hurrying off on a snorkeling trip that afternoon. So I got to the point and asked them how they met. She said he showed up at a party she had thrown one night with one of her male friends. They talked all night and each suspected that the other might be "the one." Her husband interjected that it was the first date that had been the clincher for him: "Everything we said was in sync and we just clicked, you know? We both like to act like clowns. And by the way, it was Valentine's Day that we met. I thought it would never happen to me and had convinced myself that I would be a bachelor for life, because I had been looking for so long. Right away, I started planning in my head that we would date for a year and get married in the fall." She interjected that though she'd never shared those thoughts in the beginning, she'd had them, too. She knew in her heart that it was just "meant to be."

Another example of right timing was relayed to me by a couple one evening while having dinner at my favorite restaurant. The beautiful couple sitting next to my table told me they were on Maui on a "getting-to-know-each-other-better" vacation. She was in her middle thirties, Danish, and had lived abroad most of her life until recently. She had started her career in England working for a company that did business in America. She was transferred suddenly to the Michigan office and ended up on the phone every day with a man who worked for another company. She said she loved his voice. "After a while, we just had to meet." That began their romance, and although he seemed more sure than she that they were meant for each other, she was almost there.

The psychic reading I gave them confirmed that they were indeed Divine Complements and that although their lives began on different continents, their co-created design had paved the way for her to relocate so that they could come together at the right time. I told them they should start planning for the long haul.

Each soul must achieve certain things before it is ready for its complement. Sometimes, karma with others will have to be honored and completed first. Some people will marry several times or have long-term relationships with others before the timing is right. These necessary karmic relationships often present difficult tests and trials that force them to grow psychologically and spiritually. When the karma is complete and the lessons have been learned, they will go their own way. Many times the reason long-standing relationships end is to allow Divine Complements to come together to fulfill their important promises to each other.

I had a nine-year committed relationship with a man whom I loved and who complemented me in many ways. He played out the role of Theseus in the myth of Ariadne and Theseus, and our destiny together unfolded almost to the letter of the myth. I helped him to travel deeply into the labyrinth of his soul with my thread of wisdom, compassion and care. And he reciprocated with love and friendship. We were deeply bonded, and the relationship was harmonious for five of the years we were together. We had many tests of love in the last four years, however, which centered on my adolescent daughter and a serious illness he'd developed that required surgery in the end. When he was released from the hospital after surgery to remove a diseased spleen, he left Maui without a word with his mother, who had been by his bedside and who, by the way, had never embraced me. He called a dear friend of mine from the airport asking her to let me know he was sorry about leaving us in this way but felt he had no other choice. He told her I could pick up his car at the airport and sell it. Although we had a certain amount of difficulty relating as lovers, I was not ready to let go of the relationship, because of the bonded friendship we had. However, divine timing had set the time for his exit a year before my Divine

Complement entered my life. Holding on would have been destructive to both of us.

The karmic plan between Divine Complements is the most important agreement made between two souls. That relationship cannot be denied or put on the back burner once the pot is on the stove for cooking up a lasting friendship. When the time arrives for the divine reunion, it is most likely that we are ready for the challenge.

Stories that reunite Divine Complements later in life are many. I once heard a story from a woman whose husband passed on when she was in her early sixties. Her husband's best friend had been in their social circle for years, spending time at their home, and had become almost like a member of their family. After her husband's death, they began to spend time together, fell in love and married. In truth, they were Divine Complements who had waited many years to be together through the test of loyalty to another partner. Although some might frown on a woman in her sixties who gets married six months after her husband dies, the destiny of a senior citizen is as strong as that of a 20-year-old. In the couple's eyes, they had waited long enough, no matter what their children thought. The love between Divine Complements must be given full opportunity to grow through its seasons, no matter what the age.

Fulfillment of the Stellar Promise is worth waiting for. Divine Consciousness reminds us that it is all in the stars and timed for the right moment. When the heart is ready for love, a welcome mat is put in front of the door. Until our complement arrives, our heart will be a waiting room wondering what God has in store for us. We may get all the time we need to rise from the disappointment from unkept promises of previous relationships and the unrealized expectations we'd had.

Divine Principle:
*Unconscious wounds will be brought to the surface, illuminated
in the reflection of the beloved and cast out by the love between
us.*

Many unsuspecting people fall from grace because they
have a great deal of emotional baggage in the way of recognizing their Divine Complement for who they are. Instead, they
unconsciously replicate a parental figure and project their
reflection like a holographic image over the authentic qualities
of their soul mate. They can't see clearly through their emotionally fogged glasses or through the rose-colored glasses of
their expectations. Instead, they will see Mom or Dad in the
behaviors of their soul mate, interpreting them and responding to them in the same way they did as a child. They may be
fooled for a long time until they develop enough insight to
recognize that they have created their mother and father all
over again in their own mind. The projected image may have
little to do with reality. The famous Jungian analyst Marian
Woodman said she could finally see her husband for who he
truly was only after 50 long years of marriage. Before that, she
had projected her father's image onto him, failing to see his
authentic qualities. It was a relief to know him, for the first
time, as someone other than her father.

A long legacy of beliefs and attitudes from our parents
about love and marriage will rise to the surface as one begins
to consider a good match. We may remember the advice our
mother or father gave us about finding the right man or
woman. However, a family legacy full of faulty attitudes and

beliefs about male and female roles may present real obstacles to seeing someone who is in service to our wholeness. We may fall to the temptation of wishing our childish needs were fulfilled instead of embracing someone who is good for us. Our tendency may be to try to duplicate the roles our own parents played in their relationship and to re-create our childhood experiences of a happy family or fulfill our childhood wishes for the perfect parent.

Some couples unconsciously go about dating and mating thinking that they are making conscious choices, but it is more likely that the choices are dictated by the values of their parents. Ideals of the perfect man or woman are often bound by parental influences. They can even dictate whom we fall in love with. Women all over the world idealize a strong man because their mothers did; whether he is muscle-bound or not is less significant than how much he likes to exercise his strength, control and fatherly influence. However, a woman will think she wants a man who knows his own mind who will lead her and protect her, only until the day she wants to make a decision on her own and finds herself testing the waters to see if it meets with her partner's approval. She has fallen into an unconscious pattern in which she desires a father who will shelter and protect her. Ultimately, she will have to battle his influence to regain her freedom and power as a woman. This level of psychological immaturity robs women of their complement, because they will undeniably deny someone who has integrated his feminine side and who is her equal. Someone who is sensitive, compassionate, intuitive and insightful may be deemed less attractive than a man who is rational, intelligent or macho. A man who honors his mother and womanhood might be seen as weak and a mama's boy. For such a woman, it is really her own weakness that she has deemed pathetic, and she will keep looking for a dominator to compensate for her lack of strength. She may even seek a man years older than her who looks and acts like her father, because she unconsciously wishes to continue being a child. She will outwardly seek a position as Daddy's girl, looking for acknowledgement and pats on the head from her mate.

Some women who feared their father's influence or who had fathers who were not assertive, allowing their wives to dominate them, may unconsciously be attracted to weak men because they have not had any real examples of masculine strength. They may seek men whom they can lead around and who will follow their directives without question. Fearing loss of control, they will be uncomfortable with letting men make decisions. And finding it difficult to trust that their beloveds' generosity is sincere, they will end up browbeating them instead of appreciating them.

Some women may consciously wish to emulate and recreate their mothers' beliefs about what kind of men they should marry and how their relationships should be approached. Loyalty to her mother's way may deny a woman her own intelligent choices. It may rob her of opportunities to grow beyond the limitations of her mother's patterns and beliefs. Books and women's magazines have popularized the "rules" of attracting and holding onto a good man, one who is prominent, established and wealthy. Just like Mom's advice, these guidelines lead a woman to believe she must play a game to make a man notice her, love her and ultimately consider her as a better match than the woman around the corner. Many women seek the match made in heaven based on ideals involving financial security rather than companionship and emotional and spiritual fulfillment. For generations, women have been rewarded less in their careers, and historically the financial picture for women has been bleak. Mothers genuinely want their daughters to suffer less than they did and may instill in their daughters the wish to find a generous and wealthy man to support her. (At the same time, they expect their boys to accomplish their own financial success, wishing them luck and providence.)

Faithfulness to Mom's notions obscures a woman's authentic choice of a complement, a complement who can serve her on her own evolutionary path and on whose path she can serve. Sometimes it is a woman's path to rise to equality by raising her status above a man's, attaining financial success on her own. Such a woman will land a high-paying job, as she was never meant to be financially cared for. Her evolutionary path may even require that she support her beloved financially to complete a karmic promise. She may have to drop the traditional role and expect more from her herself to fulfill that promise. In this case, to insist that the man be the breadwinner is not the evolved choice.

It is not so much the conscious choices a woman makes as her unconscious attitudes and belief systems that interfere with bringing her complement to her and accepting him once he has arrived. These subconscious patterns override the intelligence of a woman's heart, re-creating instead her mother's legacy. The recapitulation of subconscious patterns arises out of what is termed the Shadow, the force in the subconscious that is most hidden. A mother's shadow can flood the unconscious of a daughter, who, although she may not have faced the same threats to self-esteem that her mother did, will still live out the mother's inadequacies and scripts. A woman will have to peel away the layers of faulty beliefs, much like peeling away the layers of an onion, to reveal the core belief she inherited from her mother. A few sincere tears may be shed in the process of confronting the emotional turmoil of a mother's legacy. Its direct opposition to a woman's own value

and self-worth will need to be shed. The emotional strongholds will have to be brought into consciousness one by one
in the early stages of relationship in order for a woman to feel
valued and worthy of her mate. Sometimes a woman may celebrate too soon in having enlightened herself to the origins of
her patterns of attraction and will believe the work is done.
However, cognition is not consciousness. One after another,
she will continue to magnetize shadow lovers who challenge
her feminine power. She may have to make a conscious effort
for years to resist falling into the same old patterns of berating
herself and choosing lovers who neglect or abuse her. She may
find that by deeply cleansing her heart and forgiving her
mother and the generations of mothers before that she will be
liberated. She will need God's grace to support the forgiveness process and her own vigilance to change her behavior
and make more conscious choices about men.

In a man's case, emotional immaturity may keep him in
adolescence, trying to score it big with girls. He will see dating as a perpetual process of trying to find a delectable interest, a physically beautiful woman to wear on his arm, until he
matures and can accept an equal partner. He may continue the
course of restlessness and recklessness, seeking the excitement
of a new interest again and again, until he has had enough of
shallow relationships. The ideals of adolescence that permeate
our culture are certainly a difficult pressure to wrestle with,
because the culture compliments him endlessly for desiring
the *Playboy* centerfold rather than a mature bride who complements him. I was aghast while shopping the other day to see
a woman in her mid-fifties buying a *Playboy*-centerfold calen-
dar. She was obviously aware that I was staring at her from
behind. Without my saying a word, she turned to me and said,
"Oh, this isn't for me. It's for my son, who is in his late twen-
ties. He likes these." I returned home and prayed for her soul.

Such collusion and neglect in teaching her son respect for a woman's intelligence and admiration for the variety of unique qualities of beauty intrinsic to the feminine soul will send him off confident that he's on the right track with his cultural conditioning. If he wakes up, he'll blame his mother for not honoring herself and for teaching him that women are okay with being seen as sexual objects. He is likely to feel betrayed that she betrayed herself by supporting his addictions.

A man who seeks a prize, not a wife, will deny himself emotional maturity in a woman. If he *does* find a mature woman, she will probably be the type who mothers him rather than standing beside him as an equal. Because he hasn't done the soul-searching and personal growth on his own, she will deem him needing a cure and her nurturing tendencies will kick in to try to solve his problems for him.

Some subconscious patterns that a man may inherit from his father are likely to leave him emotionally disengaged and difficult to communicate with. He may deem his own emotions as shameful and embarrassing and thus may find it hard to discuss any kind of emotional need with someone closely connected to him. His emotions will be well-defended by walls that keep him from his heart and from expressing love and tenderness. He may think he has it all together, but he will never be able to figure out what a woman really wants from him when she says, "Talk to me." He may be conscientious and accomplished at work but, in a relationship, lacks confidence. He may flee with his heart and mind and eventually may even abandon the relationship if he senses the danger of entrapment.

To rise after the fall, couples may need to grow up quickly by sorting through their baggage together, and helping each other to develop insight into the patterns they carried into the relationship. They must realize that any limitations in their relationship, such as unmet needs or failed expectations, can signal a need for personal growth. They will have to take responsibility for their own shortcomings before they can expect their partners to change.

When emotional immaturity is revealed through a slap in the face, like a relationship problem or a broken engagement, we are likely to do a lot of soul-searching. Emotional and spiritual growth through development of insight may improve our outlook. We may seek professional advice through couples counseling or psychotherapy to unravel the mystery of "why do I do this over and over again?" Couples counseling can pave the way in helping Divine Complements to understand how their personal baggage can overwhelm their relationship, putting unhealthy demands on it and stopping its evolution toward the commitment to love. Too often the spiritual side of the relationship is ignored and the quest becomes one of individuation and personal growth for each individual outside the relationship. The divine and spiritual connection, the "meant to be," is now cast out of the heart in favor of a rational view that we may have to do it solo. They may come to believe, "I must have chosen an immature partner, and now I have to find another person or another focus until I am ready again for love."

I was recently watching a relationship expert on TV helping a couple solve a problem they were facing in their marriage that revolved around their complementary careers. The woman was an actress who had had significant success and recognition in Europe before she met and subsequently married her beloved. He, too, had a career in theater and filmmaking, and all was good for a time as they complemented each other's talents. Yearnings for more fame took them both to Hollywood to pursue a bigger dream. The decision seemed right at the time, as they were confident that fame and fortune would naturally follow. Unfortunately, they left a river of abundant opportunities and entered an ocean of negative currents that diminished their pride and self—esteem and brought them disappointment instead. They were having serious financial concerns because their careers had taken a nosedive.

The woman was set on returning to Europe, where she had established contacts and many opportunities to work in theatre. Her husband wasn't eager to give up the big dream to make it in Hollywood, suggesting that the two years had not been enough time for them to stand out in a highly competitive market. His wife, however, was suffering because her friends and family were in Europe and she had to work outside her profession to make a living for the two of them. She was being diminished while he waited for the big break. After exploring their desire to remain together, their desire for financial and career success and their willingness to compromise out of respect for each other, the expert offered a solution to end their suffering. He recommended a temporary separation during which the woman could return to Europe to reclaim her success and the man could remain in Hollywood to pursue his dream for a time. It would offer an opportunity to see whose way worked. He said they could set a time limit and reunite in a year or so.

They seemed amenable to the idea, probably because the expert was an expert, after all, and his compromise sounded logical. I was aghast at the therapist's lack of spiritual consciousness and his eagerness to have them work on a solution that could destroy the very fabric of their committed complementary relationship. Given that long-distance relationships create distance, not closeness, it seemed to me a ridiculous solution that they should part for even a short period and that the bond and commitment to each other would be compromised. The repercussions of her moving back to Europe without him might mean the end of their marriage. The most sacred divine promise and commitment to love, God and each other would be sacrificed for fame. I knew that when couples confront failure in achieving their goals, maybe fate had offered them a lesson in humility. The soul design seemed obvious to me. The man was to humble himself and admit that their destiny together would be best-served through his support of her career for a time. After all, she had compromised, leaving all her worldly glory behind for two years to honor his bigger dream, and it didn't work. It seemed obvious that he was to let go of his need for the sake of keeping the relationship from starving.

Temptations like fame, worldly enterprise and thrill-seeking can lead couples to abandon each other to fulfill a selfish ideal. Perhaps this man had lost sight of the big picture, the one encased in his heart. Their movie should have been titled "I Am Committed to Us" instead of "Hollywood and Fame."

Divine Consciousness suggests that complementary relationships are the sacred way in which we grow individually as well as together, helping with each other's short-sightedness, shortcomings and emotional baggage. Experts and marriage counselors need to be spiritual advisers, helping couples develop insight into what evolutionary lessons they have chosen and how they can support each other in the process of understanding and fulfilling their destiny. For those who are just entering a divine partnership, an intuitive spiritual adviser can lend credibility to the bonds of their karmic contract by validating its existence.

Divine Principle:
Rising from the fall is achieved through Divine Consciousness.

What is Divine Consciousness? It is a knowing that there is a stellar twin who was born to be with us. You can call it your soul mate, your twin soul, God's choice for you, but "Divine Complement" best describes the complex aspects of this divine union.

All the myths, fairy tales and legends about a sacred marriage between the king and queen or the prince and princess point to this magical "meant to be" experience, no matter what peril befalls the prince or princess on the way to the wedding.

❋ Cinderella's slipper fits only her. Though her stepsisters would squeeze toes and crush heels in vain attempts to force their way into the slipper, the blood revealed they were impostors.

❋ Sleeping Beauty can be awakened only by her prince. Even though she looks lifeless and unmoved, his kiss springs her to life. All previous spells are dissolved.

❋ The Little Mermaid, who must mature and grow legs by breaking free of her father's patriarchal influence, is recognized by her song as the one who saved the Prince from drowning. She is proved the authentic bride over a seductress look-alike in the nick of time to guarantee the sacred union at the altar.

❋ Even Adam and Eve were perfect complements, the virgin bride and virgin groom, put in the Garden of Eden together as God's perfect archetypes. Like two notes blended to make a beautiful song of unique harmony, they were meant to be eternally bonded and enjoy the fruits of the garden.

The consciousness that a Divine Complement exists some-where in the world for us may bring us a sigh of relief. It can take us straight to our heart, to inner truth and knowing. Or it may send us into a fantasy of two who will never argue and always agree. It may swing our emotions to yearnings. We may comb the streets to find the person who will complete us. Or we may be reminded that we have already found them and that they are in the kitchen right now preparing dinner and that there has never been anyone who nurtured us more. Then again, we may wonder, "Am I with an impostor I'll have to leave or who will leave me for their Divine Complement?" In the end, knowing a Divine Complement is out there will lead us to the epiphany that there is a "meant to be," a plan in this life to bring two together to complete a destiny of fulfillment.

Chapter 5

The King and I

Divine Principle:
The King and Queen must step off their thrones for the twin lovers to rise. They represent the perfect harmony of the creative impulse rising to reclaim the world.

When I was 10 years old, my mother took me to a live performance of the musical *The King and I*. For months afterward, I dressed up in my fanciest dresses, put on my patent-leather baby-doll shoes and waltzed around the living room with my imaginary King of Siam, singing *Shall We Dance*. I seemed to never tire of the fantasy that someday I might love someone as regal as a king who would in turn honor me.

139

At the age of 50, when the remake *Anna and the King* was released, I was the first in line at the local theater to see it. Having also seen the two other Hollywood musical productions of the show, I was anxious to see whether the dramatic version would take me to the same emotional epiphany. I was not disappointed. I was captivated, especially, by the romantic tension between Jodie Foster and Chow Yun-Fat and the movie's promise of fulfillment, everlasting love and respect of the sexes. Of course, I already knew the ending would send me running to the ladies room to wipe the running mascara from my eyes. When the scene closed and Anna departed to England, leaving the King and his children behind, I was thrown into the suffering and sorrow of the impossible dream. How could two who so complemented each other and who forced each other to grow into love fail to live happily ever after? It didn't matter in the least that Anna Leonowens' story was mostly fabricated out of a desire for respect and authorship. What mattered was that the story, fiction or not, pointed to a place in need of healing, not only within my own heart but also within the collective soul of humanity. In having been revived several times, much like a recurring dream, the story restates the unresolved conflict and dilemma of inequality that has been perpetuated for centuries.

The story takes place in Siam in the mid-19th century. Anna Leonowens is a prim and proper, widowed colonialist schoolteacher who is commissioned to the palace in Siam by King Mongkut to teach his children English. She arrives with her young son and finds herself living among the King's 39 wives and hundred-some children. She first confronts the authority of the respected monarch when she insists she be given a house outside the palace walls, as was promised her. This begins a feisty and provocative play for respect and the acknowledgment of a woman's need to be honored. The King is taken aback by her demeanor and stand-up-for-yourself attitude and comes to respect and listen to her thoughts and opinions. He falls for her sensitivities and sensibilities, and she falls for his compassionate authority. He begins to see in her the equality of a woman and realize his own desire for an equal partner. And he wonders if it is possible for a man to be completely satisfied with just one woman.

She, on the other hand, sees him as needing some good old-fashioned Christian-colonialist saving from centuries of male supremacy, challenging him and yet remaining loyal at the same time. When his rulership is threatened by a vanguard of advisers who betray him, she's right there to defend and save him and his children.

As archetypes, Anna and the King are the King and the Queen witnessing their value and worth to each other. Anna, the almost-Queen, is wise enough to understand that if she is to become respected like a Queen, she will have to do everything within her power not to lose position as an equal. The King discovers that what really matters is not that others respect him but that *she* does.

However, the story takes a distressing turn when a young princess, Tuptim, arrives on scene as the latest arranged marriage for the King. She is not happy with the arrangement, because she is deeply and passionately in love with a male consort, who is obviously her match made in heaven. Desperate to be with him, she disguises herself as a monk and escapes to join him. They are captured together and executed publicly for shaming the King and the royal court.

Symbolically, Tuptim and her soul mate represent the archetypes of the lovers who will do anything, including risking their lives, to consummate their love. Respect means nothing to them, for it is love and unity that they are truly about and what they are after. Their death symbolically represents the annihilation of the twin lovers within the hearts of Anna and the King and ends any hope for them to fulfill a destiny of love, for the love between them has been sacrificed to honor. Anna returns to England without her King at her side and there is a continental divide between them.

There is a no more meaningful and symbolic story unraveling the legacy that has often destroyed the sacred spiritual union of Divine Complements. It's no wonder that this story has been told over and over despite its inaccurate account of the real relationship between King Mongkut and Anna Leonowens. (In fact, Thailand has banned *The King and I* and *Anna and the King* because of its imperialist views, proclaiming it degrading to the authentic history of its people.) In truth, King Mongkut was in his sixties when Anna arrived on the scene, and it is therefore unlikely that they were truly Divine Complements. But the romanticized story has value in describing a condition afflicting the soul of humanity that has robbed us of the equality of the sexes and the sacred union of the masculine and feminine in each of our human souls.

Patriarchal oppression resulting in gross inequality between a man's and a woman's value has left us all with a wounded and degraded feminine soul. The feminine, the intuitive and compassionate aspect within us, has been knocked off her throne by patriarchal values and attitudes that degrade her value and limit her expression. Patriarchy disregards feminine intelligence, perceiving it as no more than irrational emotionality and therefore irrelevant to human understanding and human achievement. This attitude has robbed us of the value of our innate intuitive intelligence, the balance between intuition and reason (feminine and masculine) and of our ability to utilize and apply intuitive understanding to our daily lives. It has robbed us of our divine connection to the natural world to appreciate the sacredness of life, contributing instead to wasteland attitudes that defile nature and our relationship to it. It has forced continued inequality between the sexes and allowed us to view God only as a patriarchal King, denying us true recognition of God's unified intelligence as both King and Queen (Father and Mother).

As a result, we are dominated by a world of reason, science and the one-sided morality that denies love and elevates laws, which perpetuate the patriarchal system. Women, although more conscious now than centuries ago, are still trying to win approval from systems of authority outside their own hearts. They often find that loyalty to the patriarchy will win them more acceptance than will standing in the light of their own truth. Men, separated from their true masculinity and brilliance, turn away from honoring a woman's intelligence as equal to a man's and are pushed instead to satisfy their hunger for the feminine through lust and sexual obsession.

The psychological conflict created by the inequality between male and female relationships can emerge in the dreams of both men and women as they struggle for equality and balance within their souls. The struggle between the patriarchal king and the diminished feminine was expressed in a dream one of my students shared in one of my dream groups. She said she saw herself as a handmaiden serving a king. She was dressed as a medieval servant and was holding a large bowl of water. She knew that the King's time to step down had come, but she didn't quite know how it could be achieved. In examining the dream, I recognized the deep psychological dilemma that denied her feminine soul equality. Although consciously she took pride in her professional achievements as an educator and considered herself a liberated woman, it was only by aligning with the patriarch that she was able to achieve success in her life. Her subconscious still embraced the patriarchal archetype as superior; the King was ruling her life and diminishing her intuition, emotional intelligence and worth. It was also denying her equality with her Divine Complement; rather than embracing him as a lover, she was projecting the father she so admired as a child onto his personality.

She believed that the bowl of water held a secret and transformational power. We used an active-imagination exercise to re-enter the dream and carry it toward a natural resolution to reconcile the conflict. She saw that within the bowl was a snake. The snake, a powerful archetypal force representing her own creative power, was communicating her need to embrace the creative potentials of her sexuality. She knew that her sexuality held the key to the spiritual and creative rebirth of her feminine soul. With that rebirth, the lover archetypes could reunite and dance the balance of a unified intelligence. However, the first task was for her feminine power to rise out of suppression and servitude. This meant she needed to empower her heart to embrace every aspect of her feminine soul, especially her intuition and her creative power as a healer. Through the active-imagination process, she saw herself with the snakes intertwined with her arms, symbolic of accepting her feminine healing potentials. Accompanying this image were surges of energy through her whole body indicating that she was being transformed at a cellular level. Through the support of the circle of women who applauded her initiation, she felt rooted to the earth and empowered to use her creative power more actively in the future.

For both women and men, to bring the qualities and harmonies of the feminine out of suppression requires awakening to their spiritual power, inner beauty and creative potentials. They must cast out the darker aspects of the feminine—jealousy, rage and shame—in favor of the Queen of Hearts. As an archetype, the Queen of Hearts holds the power to restore the personality to a more nurturing, compassionate and loving level of human understanding. She sits on her throne as a humanitarian, embracing all with kindness, virtue and gentleness complementing the King of Hearts, who offers the balance of reason to her heartfelt concerns. Her wisdom guides his moral judgment, offering a new balance of shared authority.

The harmonies of masculine and feminine intelligence are also reflected in the delicate balance and synergy of the Lover archetypes. Their harmonies were seeded in the beginning to reflect the unity of the male and female aspects of God. Each of their harmonies offers huge potentials of creative intelligence brought out of spiritual dimensions and into the world. The male aspect is brilliant, logical and rational. It is the active principle, which possesses the strength of will to initiate and take action in the world. The feminine is the intuitive, creative, receptive and emotional aspect that guides and nurtures through her wisdom. The male aspect and its intelligence possess angular vision, viewing the world in lines of symmetry, while the feminine sees its round wavy definitions. Maleness constructs ideas through defining the bits and pieces that, when applied together, can bring about new forms and creations in the world. The feminine perception sees the big picture and the whole in its totality. She is less concerned with the parts and more with how everything is going to come together in balance and harmony with nature and the natural order of the universe. She is intimate with nature, intuiting its pulse at all times. She is more earthbound and therefore naturally connected to her body and the physical world. The male is orientated to the higher mind and the intellect. He is more air-oriented and is concerned with mastering thoughts and the thinking function. The male is analyzing, logical, reductionistic and deductive in reasoning, while the feminine intuitively integrates the whole in her heart through a sense of feeling. The feminine moves inwardly to gain wisdom, the masculine outwardly to gain knowledge. The feminine feels it and the masculine thinks about it.

Spiritually, the feminine moves through the dimensions of consciousness with a highly developed psychic sense. She sees into many dimensions at once and integrates her experiences into a profound body of wisdom. She holds the thread to higher states of spiritual awareness, as well as to the deeper intelligence of the soul. She traverses the labyrinth of the creative legacy of human evolution and pulls out insights and meaningful metaphorical and mythological imagery to interpret the meaning of life. The male thinks his way clear to God through constructs of the universe and hierarchies of spiritual attainment. He builds his philosophy and understanding through direct contact with the light of God. His higher intelligence ignites his mind with God's intelligence and delivers God's thoughts as insight and brilliance.

In assessing the world, it is the masculine aspect that applies reason and logic to bring about ideas that can construct and reconstruct the world. He is constantly looking at what is wrong, trying to correct and perfect it. He applies his brilliance and knowledge to new expressions that will advance humanity. And he is concerned with the practical application of a higher order of knowledge to bring the world to truth, healing it from the past separation.

The feminine, on the other hand, compassionately feels the degradation of the world. She brings to it her emotionality, comfort and love through her nurturing tendencies. She sees emotions as being in need of tending and developing so that

mankind may move toward Divine Humanness. She expresses her concern and teaches us to value nature, innocence, love
and compassion above all.

As a pioneer in analytical psychology, Carl Jung con-
tributed a great deal to our understanding of the male and
female aspects within the soul. He identified them as the
anima and animus. He developed his theory of the authentic
qualities of our higher intelligence through his exploration of
dreams, which reveal the more hidden aspects of the soul. He
divided the intelligence of the male and female into what he
called functions of intelligence, which he believed needed to
be developed and balanced within each individual for the
individual to become integrated and whole. These functions
he identified as thinking, sensation, intuition and feeling. He
further believed that people usually develop two of these
functions in combination as their primary way of perceiving
and interacting with the world. He thought of himself as an
"intuitive thinking type," characterized by strong psychic
and intuitive powers as well as the reason and logic to interpret his environment correctly. We might expect that most
people in our Western culture have been trained and educated to develop their masculine sensate and thinking functions
more than their intuitive and feeling ones. In seeking to conquer the world through logic and reason, however, Western
minds have lost the big picture, the direction of their intuition
and sensibility.

In dreams, the sun and the moon often emerge as symbolic for the male and female aspects, respectively. They offer
metaphors for spiritual understanding of these unique masculine and feminine principles. The sun represents the light of
the rational mind, whose element is fire. This fire drives the
human will. The moon offers light reflected through the darkness, representing intuitive and emotional intelligence that

can move consciousness toward human understanding and wisdom. These symbols—archetypes, really—emerge from the record of deeply imprinted material within our souls, revealed often from within our dreams and within mythology. We encounter them frequently on T-shirts as defining symbols pointing to our unconscious quest for wholeness. They may be dimmed and separated from our conscious minds because we lack understanding of the symbolic world around us.

The reflections of Adam and Eve, as the Lover archetypes placed in the Garden of Eden in a state of grace, offer us an example of the unified potentials within our Stellar Hearts before the fall. Through their co-creative design of balanced harmony in ecstatic communion with God, they could have sustained the Garden of Eden in its perfection forever had they not partaken of the fruit of the Tree of Good and Evil. However, temptation and the fall split the archetype of the lovers and set them apart. They spiraled further and further from each other into the darkness that befell them by choosing duality. As the archetypes of humanity's failings, they reflect the shadow of shame cast on each of our souls and the denial of our sacred sexuality.

The fall that was created eons ago put the creative potentials of the lovers into the deep sleep of unconscious states and repressed darkness. The split-soul program overrode our authentic matrix of unified intelligence. As a result, a creative evolution was set in motion on earth, with many periods and eras that transitioned the consciousness of humanity from matriarchy to patriarchy. The matriarchal period of humanity's evolution, ending at about 1400 BCE, taught us about the spiritual force within nature, the creative harmony that lives within everything. Great agricultural societies thrived in an era when the Goddess was honored for giving life and fruitful harvest. A patriarchal shift took place with the end of the age of Taurus and humanity saw that we could conquer the natural world, experimenting with a newly found will and belief that rationality could bring about more order, morality and greater achievements. We soon discovered how the creative force of masculine intelligence could industrialize the world. That same intelligence created a technological culture that advanced us to the stars. However, the conquering era of patriarchy has ruled beyond its season, having almost destroyed our planet through its ignorance of the balance in nature. Many of us had hoped to be further along in our evolution, closer to bringing the King and Queen to equality, whereby wisdom and reason could orchestrate together a plan to save the environment and bring peace to our world. Unfortunately, we have not learned the lessons necessary to bring about cohesion between two equally important views, one of balance and one of order. Anna and the King are living on different continents, and there seems to be little hope that the lovers within them can be revived and resurrected in time to further humanity's evolution.

It's also true that while the program we have been running incarnation after incarnation still influences us, we have always had an intact motherboard perfectly harmonized with both male and female intelligence. This unified higher creative intelligence is not separate from God but constantly unified with God's intelligence. It is located within our Stellar Heart and accessible through choosing to enter its chamber, embracing the light and the qualities of our higher male and female intelligence.

Through spiritual practice, when we make that first connection with the higher frequencies of unity within our Stellar Heart, our minds begin to open to the intuitive powers that were previously dormant. We may be flooded with images of the feminine and masculine waltzing to *Some Enchanted Evening* or emerging out of a thick, dark cloud into the light. We may delight in heightened experiences of light and harmony that awaken our senses and move us deeply to love. The feminine is the first to be revived, re-emerging into consciousness ready to blossom into qualities of love, compassion, intuition and psychic receptivity. She may be as nakedly exposed as Eve, returned to innocence, or as Cinderella freed from the ashes and cinder and resurrected to her beauty for all to witness at the ball. Then again, she may be like Sleeping Beauty, awakened by her prince with a magical kiss, or Rapunzel escaping from the castle tower to join her beloved in an apple grove. Fairy-tale images of the feminine are sometimes thought to be psychologically degrading to the consciousness of women, in that they require the masculine complement to elevate a woman's worth and fulfill the dream of "happily ever after." However, they may more accurately be interpreted as beautiful expressions of the feminine soul's awakening from repression and emerging from darkness to join a masculine complement. This resolution represents a fulfillment of the sacred spiritual union and the Stellar Promise.

Divine Principle:
Individuation means letting go of our tail fins, growing legs and walking in the world, giving voice to our vision.

One of my favorite children's fairy tales is *The Little Mermaid*. When my daughter was young, she played the video of the Disney version over and over, collected toy Little

Mermaid characters and just about every evening curled up next to me to read one of the versions of the fairy tale. It so happened that I began to value *The Little Mermaid* for its mythological significance pointing to a reemergence of feminine wisdom and intelligence into the world. As a public dream, this fairy tale holds a special promise of an evolution of consciousness toward the balance of the male and female in a sacred union.

Ariel, the little mermaid, sings under the sea and wishes every day to transform into human form. As a mermaid, she represents the unrealized potentials of feminine consciousness still held beneath the surface of human understanding and acknowledgement. As the story reveals, it was not an easy task for Ariel to make the leap from living safely in the undersea world of the unconscious to being realized in the world as an equal partner to masculine intelligence. She had to dishonor her father's will, freeing herself of service to his patriarchal influence that wished to keep her a child forever singing to his tune. Her adolescent quest for individuation required a rebellion against the very safety of her father's watchful eye and authority. She could no longer have her spirit dampened by fatherly advice and rules about where she could go, what she could say and who she could become. Challenging the patriarchal ruler is not an easy task for women or men who wish to let their intuition and emotional intelligence guide them. They may find that loyalty to the patriarch will win them more acknowledgements than will standing up for their own values and higher ideals. However, to evolve, they must slay the father archetype, the supreme dictator, that quashes the desires of the authentic self and obstructs the path to individual destiny.

Ariel had to pay a great price to grow legs and be accepted in a world of male intelligence. Her bargain was with the unconscious forces of the Sea Witch, the mother archetype, to give up her beautiful singing voice. This bargain offered her no way of expressing her authentic qualities or creativity, no way of seeing herself as having any worth in the world. Undoubtedly, without speech she would not disrupt the balance of the patriarchal world, and the world would continue to be a wasteland without the guidance of her spiritual vision and the voice of her wisdom. So, when she landed on the shore of the real world to meet her beloved masculine twin soul, she was trying without speech to win the recognition from him that she was his authentic bride. This is a heart-wrenching real-life dilemma, as many men and women silence their intuition, the guidance of their spiritual eye, as well as their emotional intelligence in order to be safe and accepted in the material world. They learn early from their mothers and fathers not to rock the boat with ideas that go against the currents of the establishment for fear that they will not gain acceptance or achieve success in life. Many men and women buy into the stagnant legacy of their mothers and fathers until an unconscious drive for unity pushes them toward a destiny of equality.

The male aspect in *The Little Mermaid* is portrayed as a solar hero named Eric. He must not be fooled by his mother's look-alike, a *femme fatale* who poses as the girl of his dreams but is really Ursula, the sea witch, in disguise. Psychologically, she seeks to hold him captive in the snare of his mother's values, qualities and charm. Representing the unconscious grip that a mother holds on her son, seducing him into denying his intelligence by seeking emotional pleasure instead, Ursula's power overrides his destiny. He makes it all the way to the altar with the impostor, and the Little Mermaid, still without a voice, can do nothing to stop him. He, however, miraculously comes out of his trance in the knick of time and slays the sea witch. Symbolically, he becomes conscious of the mother complex, which denied him an equal bride, breaking the spell that had him believing that a mother look-alike would advance him further on the royal road to happiness than his complementary partner could. He's free to choose his authentic bride, and Ariel's singing voice returns. With this transformation, Ariel's father accepts the maturation of his daughter and concedes, offering his approval for their royal wedding. Both Ariel and Eric have psychologically individuated, free of the legacy of their parental influences and spiritually unified in the sacred marriage. They are wed, and the promise of "happily ever after" is realized.

What the story of the Little Mermaid reveals is that there are subconscious forces in opposition to the union of the masculine and feminine that must be overcome. A woman or a man must become aware of the patterns of their mothers and fathers that still influence their psyche, as well as the strong archetypes within the collective unconscious that force the authentic male and female into submission. These forces emerge as voices in the dark, saying things like "You can't use your intuition, because people will think you're crazy," "You're too sensitive for your own good," "If you speak out, you will be betrayed or harmed" and "You have to honor the world and its values for what they are or you are sure to suffer." All these statements comment on the real pressures confronting even the most liberated individual to conform. They represent a strong pull to deny the harmony of the masculine and feminine in favor of a lopsided consciousness of reason, which denies the voice of spirit and the path of individual destiny.

What harms the true masculine and feminine polarities within each individual soul also harms the relationship between Divine Complements. The baggage that is carried into a relationship courtesy of Mom and Dad may be heavily weighted with values and attitudes that suppress the expression of the authentic self. A married couple may witness the same old conflicts in their relationship that were present in their parents' marriages. Our arguments may be as familiar as television reruns, as they replicate our parents' disputes. Our evolution will demand that we work them out even if our parents never did.

Instead of behaving as mature, enlightened adults concerned with the person in front of us, we may be taken back to early childhood to seek reconciliation with parental figures. This can interfere with the recognition of each other as equal and mature partners whose authentic qualities contribute to each other's wholeness.

We may discover that our partner is acting like our mother or father, controlling us as if we were a child. We will be confronted with the wounded child in ourselves seeking parental attention, reward or appreciation. Our partner will not be our equal but will have authority and power over us instead. We may find ourselves being punished or rewarded in the relationship rather than honored.

Many men and women may even seek out mother or father look-alikes. They want to be mothered or fathered more than they want respect or acknowledgment for their authentic qualities. A man may cherish his mother's comfort or even her demanding tone, still feeling the need to fulfill unmet childhood desires for love. A woman may demand that her husband become her father; rather than standing on her own, she may seek protection and approval from him. She may put demands on her husband to provide for the two of them, denying herself the equality she deserves.

If our partner possesses the qualities of either of our parents, there will be a strong attraction. The attraction is a magnetic force that in many ways illuminates the need for healing and individuation. And when those qualities are not present, they may be projected onto our partner anyway. Couples may eventually become repelled by the very same qualities that attracted them in the beginning. They may view their partners as being too motherly or fatherly for comfort, and they may be left feeling strangled or tied down.

We may be challenged emotionally when confronted with a parental figure sitting across from us at the marital dinner table. The food may be overcooked with criticism or undercooked because of neglect and avoidance. We are likely to feel starved for affection. In such a case, there is nothing nurturing or fulfilling in the activities we share with our complement, and we may find our creativity, imagination and passion stifled. The lovers will be exiled to a dungeon for wishing to express love, and we will have a great deal of difficulty convincing them to return to the bedroom for some romance.

This dynamic tension of seeking certain qualities while at the same time rejecting them can put stress on a relationship. We may be afraid that we are not seen for who we really are. We may feel as if we are being forced to play out the role of mother or father and expected to make up for the neglect that our partner felt as a child. Or we may feel forced to deny and forsake some of the parental qualities that we desire, in order to keep the relationship harmonious. These are some of the traps of projection that can fog our glasses and prevent us from seeing our partner for who they truly are. Unconscious forces will reveal the projections for what they are and help us unearth the emotional attachments of childhood so they may be reckoned with.

The intelligence of love must bring us to the truth, that there is healing to be done and that the person in front of us is not our mother or father but is instead the healer we asked for. They are perfectly endowed with just what is necessary to sort out our mother or father's values, ideas about the world and the way they viewed relationship. We will have to sort out confusing attitudes and beliefs by illuminating them in compassionate communications with our partner. Emotional immaturity must give way to understanding, insight and love. Willingness to witness our parents' style of communication in our own interactions will bring us insights and clarity. We may then make the choice to adopt loving and compassionate exchanges rather than fall to blaming and bickering. Above all we must recognize our partner's value as a complement, in pushing us toward maturity and equality in relationship.

Divine Principle:
There is a continental divide between Divine Complements that reflects the separation within the split soul. The water between them is the emotional intelligence of love that joins them again.

Most of us are by now familiar with the concept that men and women are as different as Venus and Mars in the way they view themselves, each other and the world. Men will naturally identify with the more masculine characteristics of their unified intelligence. They will gravitate toward analysis, reason and logic in making decisions. Women will more naturally identify with the feminine qualities of receptivity, emotional logic and intuition. They are likely to seek complete understanding of a situation before making their choices.

There is natural tension between these two styles of approaching life choices within Divine Complementary relationships, as men often exercise their masculine strength at the expense of women's desires for deeper understanding and emotional logic. The male ego often over-identifies with its masculine intelligence, resulting in rigidity, stubbornness, lack of compassion and unwillingness to listen to a more feminine point of view. The ego develops through its identifications. Gender identification is an important psychological integrative process and will take many years to accomplish. Some children will develop their personalities through modeling the characteristics and behavior of a parent, but most do it by expressing their innate and natural masculine or feminine traits. Later, as a person matures, the ego may struggle to maintain its identifications in the face of the constant reflection of an opposing polarity. Often, the choice will be opposition rather than embracing the complementary aspect. The result can be likened to the King and Queen archetypes acting as opponents, each trying to dethrone the other. In relationships, the ego that is overly identified with its masculine intelligence will impose its will on its partner, trying to force submission. Inequality and domination will arise, and a continental divide will develop in the relationship. A couple will fail to relate to each other until the currents of love force a new approach and change.

The evolutionary challenge is for the ego to identify more and more with the complementary aspect of the opposite polarity. Men will have to begin to identify with their intuition and emotional intelligence as much as with their masculine strength and logical side, and women with their masculine functions in order to balance their emotionality and intuition. They will soon derive self-esteem from this integration process that moves them beyond the ego strongholds that oppose their authentic unified personality. A balanced self-identity will be born.

There is a very important reason for gender identifications that goes beyond the development of a personality that is gender-specific. Men and women, as souls, choose a gender identity before coming into each incarnation so that their soul will evolve within a human personality. Through accumulative experiences, the soul is to gain an appreciation of each intelligence for its unique expression. It will learn through its chosen lessons to honor maleness and femaleness for what they have to offer. It also gains firsthand experience in having the opposite gender reflected back to it through relationship. Through the constant reflection of complementary qualities, it will begin to integrate both into its human experience.

As a man, the natural choice will be to exert male intelligence through reason and logical means, conquering old ideas and concepts and paving the way for new ones. A man will grow to understand that through sheer will and relentless perseverance, he can make a difference in his world if he aligns his ideas with his higher intelligence. He will grow to his masculine authority every time he succeeds at influencing others. And will learn to value male brilliance as a light in the world that casts out the darkness of archaic beliefs.

A woman's natural tendency will be to intuit her surroundings and give everything the love and support of her wisdom. She will evolve to be more intuitive, compassionate and in tune with the natural world, as she consistently trusts her intuition as valid. In her relationships, she will offer her intuitive guidance and support with love and compassion.

As mentioned, the psychological task for everyone is not only to use the identifications that are natural for our gender but also to embrace and integrate the opposite polarity as well. Evolution will be not only pulling us toward seeking equality in our relationship, as two halves making a whole through marriage, but also seeking balance within our individual soul to unify our intelligence as both masculine and feminine.

We will use the number 22 in numerology as the number of soul and spiritual mastery. It represents the union of opposites dancing together in perfect harmony encoded in the template of love. This spiritual mastery is an achievement in using both intuition and reason to fulfill our dreams as well as our individual destiny. Eric and Ariel arrive dressed for the wedding within each of us, and we are married to ourselves complete and whole.

Accomplishing that is not easy, because the forces of male intelligence often outweigh the feminine. As we remember from *The Little Mermaid*, Eric had already been in the real world with legs before Ariel made the transformation from mermaid to human. As the masculine of the collective, he had gained competence in exerting his will on the world for eons while Ariel was swimming around with a tail fin, an evolutionary vestige of her immaturity. Ariel, as Venus emerging from the sea, may find that she is not only in opposition to Mars but also in a room full of other male planetary forces that oppose her. Saturn, Uranus, Jupiter, Mercury, Neptune and Pluto, all male archetypes, converge on her consciousness, pushing her to the limit to defend her feminine intelligence. She must rise to the love and beauty she is meant to express. We can imagine that it might be like a woman being in a room with seven men, some encouraging her authentic power while the others oppose her. The planets' pull on the female intelligence can be seen as an evolutionary charge to resurrect feminine qualities within each individual. All these planets will fine-tune us as their opposition tests and strengthens the feminine will. This will happen for women as they try to assert love's intelligence in the world and for men as they face the tensions of patriarchy, which may have pushed them to deny the qualities of intuition, emotional logic and compassionate caring.

When the feminine emerges as royal as her masculine counterpart, she will have to honor that she can't do it all without him. Intuition without logic and reason will never arrive at an understanding of the full scope of spiritual truth, nor will it change anything in the world. We would have an individual with wisdom who is unable to see how it can be applied to a world that desperately needs intuition to heal it from a legacy of inequality. Without the masculine sense of order, there would be chaotic thinking. The personality could fall into confusion or even psychosis if the feminine psychic field becomes flooded with unwanted emotional content and thoughts from others. Confusion is common with intuitive/feeling types, who, although highly psychic, may have difficulty achieving enough clarity to correctly interpret what they perceive. The natural tendency of the feminine will lead her to the inner world to sort out the wounds that separate her from her maleness. She will have to retrieve the masculine and heal him in order to individuate and achieve clarity.

The balance and harmony must be a dance of equality in which the masculine and feminine avoid stepping on each other's toes. We usually imagine male intelligence leading this dance while the feminine follows. However, this is a reversal of what is natural and even logical. The feminine intuitive function must be the guiding principle leading the masculine forward to fulfill the destiny of the individual. The feminine will receive the signs and messages from other dimensions, describing and interpreting them with her heart. She will communicate them as wisdom. The masculine will further analyze them, make sense of them logically and begin to create constructs through which her visions can be applied to life. He will then pursue her visions, actualize and materialize them. The reverse would prove debilitating to both. The male would be blindly thrusting his logic, reason and will, moving the world to suit his ideas without guidance or the ability to see the big picture. He would achieve what is reasonable and miss what is intended to be his path. The feminine would be running behind him, trying to influence him by inserting her vision after the fact. Her contribution would be meaningless other than to point out mistakes that have already been made. This reversal has been more the rule for most who value masculine intelligence as supreme. And women are often the first to criticize men when they have proved themselves ignorant and resistant to feminine models for the world.

To envision the harmonized intelligence of the male and female, imagine an artist before his canvas. He looks inward for the subject of his painting. With feminine intuition, he brings it into definition. He has tapped into the imagery of the subconscious, and other worlds emerge with content. He then applies what he knows technically to bring the object of his vision into form. He may analyze elements of light and dark to give the painting depth and illumination. He will rely on his male intelligence to choose the right brush, color and strokes to create the effect he wants. From beginning to end, the work of art will be created through the intertwined harmonies of two unique intelligences, and the finished painting will reflect this union. Moving from intuition to reason, feeling to impression and then into form, the finished painting is visionary art created through balanced intelligence

We have opportunities each and every day to use both our feminine intuitive gifts and our masculine logic to bring our personal dreams into manifestation. The intelligence of our higher selves manifests its intelligence to create experiences that help us to regain the balance. Life will offer a magical interplay of creativity, synchronicity, magic and grace. Our days may be filled with synchronistic events, some of them tests that ask us to trust our feminine intuition more in following a trail of clues to the fulfillment of our desires. With our unified intelligence, we will create good things as long as we stick to a vision of our divine purpose and destiny. Bridging the gap between the two polarities is often easier said than done. We must trust intuition without abandoning reason.

Our Divine Complement will naturally model our least-expressed or repressed side, offering their example to witness and learn from. Through the sheer fact that we are spending our days and nights with them, we will naturally integrate more and more of their intelligence and traits over time. This process will come through some conscious effort, but most of it will be accomplished at unconscious levels through the blending of our harmonies. Eventually, we may even take pride in having bridged most of the gap between the masculine and feminine aspects of our souls and are likely to give credit to our relationship with our Divine Complement for having brought us home to unity.

Chapter 6

Complementary Match

Divine Principle:
Our complementary partner is in our life to help us grow potentials that we have deep inside but have not yet mastered.

Our Divine Complement is our twin, a spiritual brother or sister. They have a great deal in common with us and are matched in every way to reflect the buried qualities of our internal wholeness. Divine Complements reflect to each other their unique intelligence, aptitudes, talents and styles of relating. They may have very different styles of approaching and solving the day-to-day problems that arise, but most of the time they will arrive at a similar conclusion. Just like with brothers and sisters, conflicts and differences in opinion are apt to arise from time to time. During the course of the relationship, how the differences are viewed will determine how successful the relationship will be.

Opposites attract, without question. Whether a couple meet in the middle with respect for each other's equality or battle each other trying to force submission depends on how enlightened they are and how willing they are to learn from each other. Our complement's approach may seem to be out in left field, while we're standing on home plate waiting for the outcome. They may seem to worship the sun, while we flirt with the moon. Sometimes we feel as if we are living on two continents so far apart that it would take a miracle to see eye to eye. While we are concerned with finances at tax time, our partner wants to go skin diving, to the movies or out for a sunset walk. Or they may prefer having a room full of friends at home every weekend, when all we want to do is curl up with a good book and enjoy some downtime. We may begin to see our partner as being in opposition to our plans rather than supporting our vision for the future. If there's no appreciation for the differences within a relationship, tensions will mount and emotional discord will follow.

What happens for some couples is that one partner will give up trying to change the other's mind and conform to most of the other's desires. The equality in the relationship falls apart and needs won't be met. Emotional distancing can result, which will eventually put an ocean between them. The needs of one may dominate the relationship and neither will be fulfilled in the end, because they didn't respect themselves or each other enough to honor the way of balance.

The differences between two who are perfectly matched may bring some couples to the epiphany that they would actually rather live under the same roof with someone who is different from them than with someone whose nature is identical to theirs. I met a couple recently who credited the likes and differences between them with keeping their relationship equal, interesting and noncompetitive. They had been married for over 30 years, having met when they were only 5 years old playing as friends in the same neighborhood. It was a "meant to be" reunion when they met again in high school quite some time after their families had moved away from their common neighborhood. They were obviously meant to spend the majority of their lives together, having been deposited on the stage of life side by side in early childhood as spiritual brother and sister. The man had a strong set of values about how children should be raised, what an ideal society should consist of and what the institution of marriage should be about. He was very opinionated and, by most standards, moral and insightful. They agreed they teamed together quite well to parent their two children because they were bonded by a set of values they both honored. They were in total agreement about most things because their values were the same. However, their styles of relating and their personalities were very different. She was in no way as opinionated as he was, nor did she feel as comfortable baring her soul to everyone. He, on the other hand, had all the right answers and loved sharing his ideas and philosophies openly. He was a lion and she was a lamb. He remarked that if she had been too much like him, he would have killed her a long time ago. She was accustomed to allowing him the center stage, as long as he didn't interfere with her domain. She liked the fact that he left the house to her and did not interfere and that he took care of traditionally male things such as maintaining the cars and the finances. At one point in the conversation, she lifted her head to say she didn't have to prove she was a liberated woman, because she just was. They were the most harmonious couple I could ever wish to meet, but I wondered when she would learn from his lead that her opinions counted and that she had as many opinions to offer as he did. Instead, she allowed the light to shine on him while she remained in the shadows.

As spiritual brother and sister, a couple enters the relationship reflecting to each other the masculine and feminine intelligence of their souls. Usually women carry the feminine attributes of intuition and emotionality, reflecting their emotional intelligence to their male complement, while men offer their masculine brilliance for their feminine partner to marvel at. However, sometimes the reverse is presented in complementary relationship, demonstrating that men can be just as or even more intuitive and compassionate than women and that women can be orientated toward logic, feeling most secure with their thinking and sensation functions.

I met a couple honeymooning on Maui who shared with me the complementary characteristics of each other's personalities over a cup of coffee. The woman said she believed their differences were quite obvious to everyone around them. She described her husband as laid-back, calm, honest and a good communicator. He expressed emotions easily, which she said helped her to feel comfortable in the relationship. His name was Earnest, a name she laughingly said reflected his authentic character. On the other hand, she described herself as gregarious, serious, impatient most of the time and in a hurry to get things done. She liked initiating things immediately and actively pursued her goals with a more masculine, headstrong approach. He was as serious about his profession, but his style was to let the world come to him rather than to pursue it. His view reflected the receptive intelligence of the feminine, allowing for life's enfoldment of the greater plan. He said he envisioned them being married for 10 years before having any children. She wasn't exactly in agreement about having to wait that long and glared at him as if he was crazy to think they would wait 10 years to start a family. She did agree that they needed some time to lay the foundations of their relationship before opening the door to little ones, though.

A couple's complementary qualities and styles may blend nicely as they collaborate to fulfill their vision together. Blending strengths will be the way they create a more purposeful and meaningful life.

A few years ago, I was counseling a lesbian couple who had a lot of emotional baggage and needed to appreciate the perfect match of qualities they offered each other. They were Divine Complements who had chosen in this life to both identify with the feminine aspect of their souls. They had a beautiful soul-to-soul connection and a love bond that was nurturing and fulfilling. Their personalities were very different. One was a playful free spirit, while the other sought order and organization and tended to overwork herself. They had collaborated to get a business venture off the ground, one in which their creative talents could come together. Their co-creative harmony seemed to manifest all the opportunities they dreamed of, especially in the beginning. They traveled to Bali to have clothing designs made and imported them to the U.S., selling them at a local swap meet. Within two years, they had opened a retail store and their designs were in stores all over the country. Their different but complementary styles and talents had come together to make the business a successful one. The business offered them an opportunity to travel and play, satisfying the personality of the one and teaching the other that work could be a fun adventure. The free spirit was meant to learn quickly that organization and a stronger work ethic were what she needed to develop to fulfill her goals.

Becoming enlightened to the need for growth through integrating our partner's complementary qualities is an important acknowledgement. A major task will be not only to use each other's strengths to achieve the means but to assimilate and incorporate our partner's qualities as the means for an inner transformation. The ultimate aim is to integrate as many of our partner's positive qualities as possible while maintaining our own. Through witnessing their strengths and positive qualities, we will notice immediately that what is being demanded from us is to unmask our own hidden potentials and suppressed qualities.

As spiritual brother and sister, appreciation for the differences and unique qualities that our complement brings to the relationship is an important acknowledgment. Embracing our partner's complementary approach will reward us with three stars on our first report card in the classroom of brotherly and sisterly love. Our complements may teach us how to become more steadfast on our goals and how to assert our will and intelligence more. Or they may show us that a little more playtime and less nose-to-the-grindstone time will get us more from life. In this way, they may help us return to the playground of innocence where the divine child awaits to point out the magic that is everywhere. Letting go and nurturing the relationship may be just the achievement we need in order to put our goals into perspective. On the other hand, if we needed to learn in a hurry that hard work is what will get us to the top, our complement might bring to the relationship a strong work ethic to marvel at and emulate. We are not meant to use their strength by letting them do all the achieving—we are meant to get up to speed and match some of their drive.

Sometimes this need for growth in our personality may challenge us, and we may believe we can never match our partner's intelligence, achievements or talents, but our soul demands that we at least try. Lack of self-esteem may turn into stubbornness, and we may try to fight the challenge instead of embracing it as a growth lesson. Many couples label each other's strengths as weaknesses because they can't imagine how their approaches will work. In doing so, they may have missed the whole point of a complementary relationship: that it's meant to challenge our views, beliefs and attitudes. Our soul mate is in our life to help us achieve personal mastery, not to deter us.

Our Divine Complement may arrive at the door of the relationship reflecting a higher level of spiritual development than our own. They may have been raised with a good foundation and understanding of God's love, or they may have brought this understanding forward from previous incarnations. In this case, it is likely they had made an early agreement in the form of a karmic contract that insisted they guide us to God and toward love's intelligence in this incarnation. For them there is no question as to God's role in the relationship, and it will be their job to offer their faith as an example to us.

Some couples find that their spiritual orientations and persuasions, although different, are not a big issue in the relationship. Jews marrying Catholics and Protestants marrying Buddhists are common in our modern age. A couple's spiritual purpose together may be to sort out the baggage of spiritual beliefs or religious ideologies with which they were raised and to arrive together at the truth, that their divine partnership is the proving ground of Godliness. They may realize that they don't have to adopt a particular religious orientation, convert or claim religion as the path to God. They just need to add God to the equation of their relationship.

The intelligence of love helps us to become enlightened to the big picture of our relationship's purpose. Our complementary partner is in our life to help us grow into potentials we have deep inside but have not mastered. We may need to develop some of their strength, their sensitivity or their positive outlook to augment the way we view ourselves and our own future.

Our complement's positive attributes and qualities will be reflected back to us daily, along with the less-than-positive behaviors we may wish to disown. If we think our partner is too wishy-washy or too bossy, for instance, they may actually be giving us a picture of how others may view us. Our disowned parts will usually be a source of agitation when they are reflected back to us. Recognizing our imperfections is a lot harder than recognizing them in someone else. We may be blind to how we do and say some of the same things that aggravate us about our mate. The reflection of negative behaviors in our partner should keep us honest with ourselves and push us to make improvements in our own personalities before demanding that they change. Fortunately, the vast majority of what is reflected back will be some of the same qualities that we wish to be cherished and honored for. By appreciating our partner's finer traits, we may even grow to love ourselves more.

Divine Complements are meant to learn from each other. Relationship is their school. Every day we enter the classroom of relationship and are offered creative experiences that encourage psychological and spiritual growth. The classroom of relationship will lay out in plain view some of our character weaknesses, not only those that directly affect the relationship but those that interfere with our self-worth and personal achievements. Our mate's job will be to point them out compassionately so that we will be encouraged to work on them. Their insights can point us toward more and more self-evaluation. We may surely notice that they always seem to know what our shortcomings are, especially the deepest, darkest parts of our personality. Through our partner's loving attention, intention and constructive help, our dark parts will be illuminated so that we can grow to understand their source and let them die. Sometimes our weaknesses may test their patience, understanding and compassion.

Love doesn't necessarily approve of everything we do, but it does improve us. We may not get everything we want in a partner, but we will usually get what we need to grow to divine humanness within the relationship. Our wish lists of personal ideals will have to be discarded to accommodate the divine list that was written long before this incarnation. It represents our karmic promise and contract with our Divine Complement, honoring both of our individual needs for personal evolution. In it, we described the kind of classroom in which the relationship would begin, what karma we would have to make up for, and the appropriate kinds of lessons and even hardships we would have to endure to grow. Spiritual mastery and divine humanness are the ultimate achievements placed in front of us. Our contract unfolds as fateful experiences that test our earnestness and devotion to the spiritual path of relationship. They may also from time to time test our patience. We are meant to develop spiritual awareness in order to notice life's meaningful plan and to understand that a spiritual relationship brings meaning and purpose to our existence. Illumination of our contract can help us to identify and understand what we are expected to learn through the course of our relationship. Through contemplating circumstances in our relationship, we may become aware of the lesson at hand—ideally while it is happening—so that we can gain insight before we make cruel mistakes.

Many of us need to value ourselves as equal partners in relationship. Therefore, our lessons often force us to appreciate the necessity of equality with our partner. A woman's emotional and intuitive intelligence is different from a man's analytical and rational thinking, but it holds as much value. A woman should stand her ground, for example, when she intuits that her husband's reasonable-sounding financial expectations will fall short. She will have to give voice to her intuitive predictions even in the face of his reasonable claims.

Some people interpret equality to mean separate bank accounts that hold equal amounts of money. A friend of mine had always set her sights on attracting a man who would match her earning power if not surpass it. However, all her long-term relationships were with men who failed to be providers. They could never match her earning power. Time and time again, she found herself the primary breadwinner, supporting someone who didn't value her. She became so disturbed by this pattern that she set out to will it away by repeating affirmations and vowing that she would never settle for less than a man who could support her for a change. It never worked. Her lesson was realizing the worth of a woman, through the experience of manifesting materially and offering support to the men she loved. When her Divine Complement came into her life, he presented the same scenario. His lesson was one of humility. He was meant to understand the worth of a woman who could support his growth. The plan offered the two of them opportunities to learn respect for each other outside the financial arena.

Illuminating the lessons brings us to a platform of higher consciousness. I call it the 50-foot perspective. We will recognize that a creative spiritual force is right behind us, pushing and forcing growth, especially when we are falling to destructive patterns and negative thinking. It will ask us to change our mind and heart and open to higher guidance. We will be drawn toward our hearts and away from logic, especially when we think we already have all the answers. The light will shine on our imperfections at times when we need to introspect and will comfort us when we need more understanding. We will become enlightened to the meaning of our existence and to relationship's purpose of bringing us back to the ground of love's intelligence, time and time again. The intelligence of love will help us to put each other's patterns and imperfections into perspective and will urge us to support each other's healing. As we do, we will learn what it means to be divinely human, nurturing and supporting through brotherly and sisterly love. The intelligence of love will redeem our soul and move us to the next grade in our journey toward graduation.

The development of our feminine side is important to maintaining our focus on the big picture, especially when the little things seem insurmountable. Feminine intuition will lead us out of the darkness by illuminating the obstacles we need to remove to return to love. We rely on feminine understanding for making intimate contact with our partner, sensing any emotional turmoil that resides in our beloved's heart or beneath the consciousness of his or her understanding. Through images, visions and dreams, we can receive clues to the secrets that they may need our help to uncover.

I received a dream today from a dreamer who was deeply concerned about his beloved. In the dream, the dreamer was in a house that was mysteriously dark and that he described as a kind of purgatory. He was exploring it because his wife had moved into the house recently. He found her asleep on the bed and tried desperately to awaken her, but she was so deeply asleep that she seemed to be under a spell.

What this dream revealed was that his beloved had entered an emotionally dark place, a self-created purgatory that might even signify a deep depression. His desperate attempt to awaken her undoubtedly represented his futile attempts to reach her emotionally and his frustration at being unable to help her. His task would be to rescue her from her personal crisis through sharing the insights he had received from the dream. Through the intelligence of love and the intuitive insights he could offer her now, she could be brought into the light of a new understanding and begin her healing process.

Every time we lead our beloved out of the darkness of unconsciousness by illuminating their secret world—their grief, sorrow, resentment or anger—we are demonstrating the intelligence of love. This intelligence moves the relationship to deeper levels of intimacy and sharing. We must be willing to enter their darkness without fearing that its current will pull us under or that we will lose our grasp on our rational self. We must balance what we know about our partners and what we think they need with what they say they need from us. We must give what our intuition guides us to give, and that may be a little of both. By doing so, we are compassionately caring for the one we love the most and bonding intimately at emotional and spiritual levels.

Divine Principle:
Value each other, not what you think.

Some couples enter into their relationships with different sets of values from their partners'. Topics such as social consciousness, environmental consciousness, family, morality and God all are subjects of opinion. Some may regard materialism as the key to happiness, while their humanitarian partners want to give everything away to charity. They will have to sort out what is more important, their values or the value of their relationship, if they find themselves arguing for hours about world hunger.

Personal values are developed out of our experiences and will be influenced by the generation's social and cultural views. We may have to mull through a whole set of values handed down to us by our parents and by the generation before. As we develop morally, we may shed some of our parents' social and cultural views to incorporate our own ideas. The values we stick to will influence what we are likely to offer our own children as morals to live by. We may have developed our set of values from insights we have gained about the meaning and purpose of life and think that our partner should agree wholeheartedly. And we may have a very sound idea of what might make the world a better place, but our partner may sound off in disagreement.

Differing values can challenge a couple, especially when one's values oppose the other's. While the twain may never meet, they don't have to be in constant opposition. Accepting our partner's values may be the very thing we need to do in order to value our partnership and to appreciate the other's point of view. It doesn't mean we must be in total agreement with them when their values oppose ours. It means that we honor that their values are as important to them as our values are to us.

A staunch conservative married to a liberal may prove an interesting match to outsiders looking in. We might imagine that their living room would become a combat zone at election time, with propositions and platforms being argued and tempers flying. And we might wonder why complements would remain under the same roof when their values differ so much.

Some psychologists and clergy members might argue that if there are not enough common values, a relationship is destined to fail. They might maintain that it would not be a good idea for a couple to think they could change each other's mind about things that are important to them. However, evolution of consciousness is the soul's task in each lifetime. To think that sticking to a set of family values that have outlived their worth to society is an honorable decision is not honoring the need for spiritual evolution. There are values that are better aligned with higher truth and divine consciousness than others are. Cultural values are not the benchmark for successful evolution, but true spiritual values are.

The reason we might find ourselves in a complementary relationship with someone whose values oppose ours is that one of us is meant to evolve and change the direction of our thinking, as well as our heart. It may have even been included in our karmic contract that we needed to evolve in the direction of higher truth in this life. Our destiny plan also may have deposited us into a family whose legacy and values contradict God's laws, challenging our heart to address them. Our task is to individuate from this legacy and grow to spiritual maturity. We would, of course, need help in dismantling our biases to embrace a higher truth. Our Divine Complement may have agreed to be the one to honor our need for a shift in consciousness by offering values that represent higher understanding as examples to honor and adopt. Therefore, a liberal trying to sway his partner's political beliefs in the direction of humanitarian concern may have his work cut out. He may have to strongly address greed as a villain who wishes to steal the authentic life of his partner and their partnership. They may have every right to expect that their partner get enlightened to the truth, despite how hard it is to let go of a set of beliefs that have worked for them time and time again.

I recently read a biography by George Burns titled *Gracie: A Love Story*. In it, Burns reminisces about his relationship with Gracie Allen, his wife, comedy partner and Divine Complement. They were together for 40 years until she died in 1964, and their relationship was full of stories. They launched their joint career in the 1920s as standup Vaudeville comics. They then moved on

to radio, the movies and television and were extremely successful in achieving fame in all these venues. Their relationship was
truly about admiration and love despite the fact that they had
different values. Allen was raised Irish-Catholic and was devoted to her faith. Burns was Jewish, which could have been a problem if they had valued their religions, more than each other, as
their path to spiritual attainment. It was clear that Gracie and the
appreciation of Gracie was George's path to higher consciousness. She was the goddess he worshipped, and through her he
discovered the essence of God's love. She set her religion aside
to marry George in front of a justice of the peace, rather than in
church. And George put his religion aside to join Gracie when
she was invited to a private meeting with the Pope. He also felt
fine about sending their adopted children to Catholic schools
and to Mass on Sunday. Gracie never liked fame as much as
George did but agreed to pursue a career in show business
despite her reservations and what he called her microphone
phobia. George would push her to meet each opportunity that
would further their career together, and he says he never mind-
ed that the public wanted Gracie and not him. "After all, she was
the whole act," he said more than once. Gracie valued family life
and had set her heart on retiring early. George could have gone
on forever feeding Gracie lines to respond to with her illogical
logic and ditsy comic relief. When she thought it was time for
her to retire, George set aside his desire to work to be with
Gracie during their last years together. Life rewarded them
both, and it was clear at least to her that their life was no longer
about show business. She had helped her beloved to evolve
enough to appreciate a woman's ability to know when it's time
to stop working so hard and start enjoying the rewards that life
has given.

George and Gracie's spiritual persuasions and priorities
regarding career and family were not sources of argument.

That was probably because of the admiration and appreciation they had for each other's views. Each embraced the values of the other for what they could offer their marriage and their theatrical team. The way they worked out difficulties and differences of opinion was to try to fulfill each other's needs. It worked well for them. From George's description of life with Gracie, I could assume his divine purpose with her was to love one woman, under God, and to present her to the world to love also. Her purpose was to add the punch lines so that the rest of the world could appreciate that it's a woman's answers that make her husband's questions worth asking. George lived to hear Gracie's answers to his love. As a comedy team, they were the nuts and bolts perfectly fitted, showing the world the funny stuff of Divine Complementary Comedy. They were a superior example of marital fulfillment through complementary relationship.

Dívíne Príncíple:
The world offers multiplicity and variety, and there are many ways of perceiving each piece.

George Burns says often in his book that Gracie's taste for fashion and glamour was perplexing to him. He poked fun at her need for a few too many silver centerpieces for their dining-room table, to which she could never deliver a meal she had cooked herself. He also teased her about the many fur pieces she collected and seldom wore. But he appreciated her desire for extravagance even though he was satisfied with a lot less. His motto was, "If it makes Gracie happy, then I'm happy." She used to say, "Look at what George bought me," to her friends after a shopping spree at her favorite store, Saks, even though he never shopped a minute with her. Actually, she was equally responsible for their financial success, but she made it known that she considered him the generous provider. For Gracie, it wasn't the article of clothing that was the gift, it was George, and she wanted her friends to know how much she appreciated him.

Differing personal tastes are much easier to accept and even to admire than values. Whether it be with regard to music, home furnishings, a vacation destination, food or clothes, a partner will learn that his "match made in heaven" may have another idea of what is heavenly. Sometimes I enjoy watching a show called *Design for the Sexes*. Couples negotiate and compromise their styles and tastes with the help of an interior designer who may have to play psychologist to get them to agree on a room design that suits their needs and addresses each of their personal tastes. The more the couples disagree, the more interesting the show proves to be. Compromise always seems to be the solution the interior designer is after. Both members are expected to give in somewhat to the desires of the other. The word "compromise" suggests that each has to lose something to keep the other happy. This solution lacks the intelligence of love and divine human understanding. Those who can admire the tastes of their partners demonstrate a higher consciousness. They know that "different" teaches them to appreciate more of what life has to offer, that there's a whole world of experiences to explore and enjoy that have not yet been tried. Learning to enjoy as many as possible is good for the soul. In most circumstances, combining tastes will end the compromise we feel in keeping our complement happy.

Our Divine Complement may open us up to a whole new world of experiences and introduce us to new tastes to savor.

We may not choose to live in the wilderness as our partner might wish, but we may develop an appreciation of nature through our relationship, so that a summer vacation out at the cabin becomes a mutual desire.

Some people become offended when their partners try to impose their personal tastes on them. "That shirt isn't a good color for you. Try this one." "But my favorite color is blue." And so on. Many will interpret such a suggestion as a slap in the face and grumble under their breath for hours before exploding with something like, "I'm tired of you making all the decisions about where we going for dinner and what color shirt I should wear." The partner, if equally immature, may respond, "You never like what we are eating anyway, so what difference does it make? And blue clashes with my outfit tonight." In other words, "I can never please you," or "Nothing pleases you" or "You won't honor me and my choices." What was offered innocently may be interpreted as demeaning or insulting. An inaccurate interpretation of a gesture of love will erupt into a series of sour notes that can last for hours, days and if repeated, for an eternity. The way out is the intelligence of love. Or a little George and Gracie comedy hour. "Gracie, why are you wearing a full-length fur coat? It's July." "Because you bought it for me George, and we live in Beverly Hills now. It's always July."

Chapter 7

Sacred Lovers

Divine Principle:
Sacred lovers reside in a dimension above and in the dimension
below—sexual communion is consummated in the middle.

Sacred lovers dwell within all of us. They are twin archetypes that coax out our sexual nature. They emerge reborn to enliven us each time we share love through intimate experiences with our Divine Complement.

Sexual intimacy is a natural way of expressing love in divine complementary relationship. Intimate sexual experiences with our complement nurture the love we have for each other and help us to bond emotionally and spiritually. They deepen our connection and heal the core shame that corrupts sexual intelligence. Sacred sexual communion is a spiritual experience of the body, mind and spirit that touches the light and power of God. Through sexual communion with our beloved, we can raise our consciousness to the spiritual dimensions of love and experience the ecstasy of God's creative pulse.

Our sexuality is a natural condition that is as much a spiritual experience as a human drive. Sexual intelligence runs through our bodies by way of an intricate physiology. It's true we're wired for sex, with erogenous zones that stimulate our sexual intelligence into an eruption of creative energy, expanding our intimate experiences into orgasmic states. This intelligence responds to even the subtlest emotional tones of love's conversation, sensual touch and other emotionally bonding experiences with our mate.

Sexual intelligence is consciousness. It lives both in the body and outside it. Its energy is fluid and moves as currents in a creative field that extends just beyond our energy body. Sexual attraction occurs when our partner's sexual intelligence touches us within the field of intimacy.

Strong emotions create experiences within the body that can stimulate our sexual appetite or suppress our desires. Our emotional body can engage or retract as sexual desire and intimate play confront our fears and insecurities. Fear can make us fly out of our bodies, losing touch with our sensuality and passion and robbing us of pleasurable sexual experiences. As a result, we feel disengaged and disconnected from our partner during lovemaking and disinterested in sex.

Fear of intimate sexual contact is common to the human condition and between Divine Complements. Some fears amount to shyness, while others are deeply embedded and seem to have lives of their own. Subconscious fears lie in the darkness of the underworld and suppress sexual desire. They turn down the volume of our spiritual sexual energy and suppress the sexual vitality in the body. The result, for some couples, is that they are seldom in the mood for sexual contact. Some lose their sexual appetite altogether, living as celibate brother and sister without the joy of sexual intimacy for years. In cases like these, the sacred lovers are buried in the underworld, listless and lifeless until they can be resurrected through intelligent loving experiences.

Subconscious fears surrounding our sexuality can emerge in dreams. One of the most common themes in dreams revealing deeply rooted sexual fears is that of a confrontation with snakes. Dreamers often report dreams of snakes under the bed, in the closet or in the basement. In the dreams, they may fear being bitten or may actually be initiated through a bite from a snake. In most cases, the dreamers try to run away or get the snake out of the house in some way. However, if they befriend the snake it will teach them something about the nature of their sexuality and how to cultivate it as healing power. The snake, a powerful archetype, represents our innate sexual intelligence. It emerges in dreams to reveal our sexual condition as well as to remark on our sexual conditioning. If cultivated, our sexual energy will rise as a huge snake of primal sexual and spiritual power, opening up sexual centers in the body and purifying them. Purified sexual intelligence expands our consciousness into the divine and toward more sacred experiences with our sexuality. The sacred lovers rise from their coffins and emerge reborn to dance in the vibrancy of their sexual union. Our desire for intimacy and sexual contact within the relationship will increase as old snake skins of sexual conditioning are shed. We can then incorporate healthier attitudes about our lovemaking experiences, increasing our sexual drive even more. Through the cultivation of our sexual intelligence, our lovemaking with our Divine Complement will become a more beautiful and enjoyable experience.

Divine Principle:
The sacred spiritual dimension of sexuality liberates us from the conditioning of shame and raises our sexual vibration into the dimensions of God.

Our sexual intelligence has ties to our spiritual condition. We have been corrupted by a legacy of shame that has its roots in the soul and in the DNA. For humanity, the sacred lovers are in fact wounded lovers from the onset, having been cast out of primordial perfection. After the fall, we denied ourselves the knowledge of the miracle of our spiritual and sexual intelligence. A veil of mystery separated us from the internal design of integrated sexuality between androgynous lovers. The lovers within each one of us, like the mythological lovers Adam and Eve, were denied the garden of creative possibilities that our God/Goddess selves could create. Not only were we separated from the lovers within, but we were denied access to the Bridal Chamber, where the communion with our twin souls was deeply imprinted. The collective wound has been carried into every incarnation of humanity's evolution. Only through the resurrection of sacred lovers, like Adonis and Aphrodite, could we understand the oversoul's immense potentials to unite with God through that most sacred sexual experience, hieros gamos.

The expression of our individual sexuality is necessary to our wholeness and happiness. Sexual awareness helps us to understand our desires and hunger for intimate contact. Too many of us are separated from our bodies and have little awareness of our sexuality outside our relationships. We may be intimate with our partners through lovemaking, sensitive to their needs, but too often have little regard for our own sexuality outside the lovemaking experience. We believe that being sexy is synonymous with youth, looking good and flirting, failing to recognize that the chemistry we are seeking is within our own bodies and communicated through an invisible field to our mate. We must become sexually and sensually aware, embracing all our sexual desires as natural and important to our bodies' health, our emotional well-being and our spiritual evolution.

Conditioning influences the way we feel about our individual sexuality, how we feel about sex in general and how we perform sexually with our partner. Conditioning often overrides our innate sexual intelligence, blocking and depressing the flow of our vital spiritual energy. As children and adolescents, we consumed the sexual attitudes of our mother, father, grandmother and grandfather. We then translated their attitudes into our own belief system and into mind-sets about our sexuality. Some of what we experienced were their unconscious hurts, violations, neglect and shame carried over from their own family's legacy. In a way, we were infused with memories that were not our own. The discord corrupted our DNA, overriding the intelligence of the oversoul, and depressed our sexual intelligence, putting it into a field of sexual disharmony. The poison of shame clouds our emotional bodies, dousing the passionate flame of sexuality with waves of polluted emotions. The shadow of shame can brew deep within our hearts and within our sexual centers, making it difficult to become aroused or to enjoy sensual and sexual contact. We may perform well, but inside we may harbor a mind full of shameful attitudes that harm our spiritual innocence and make us believe we must conceal our sexiness and desires from others, even our mate.

The spiritual nature of our sexuality has been neglected and even negated by cultural imperatives about sex, which suggest that sexual potency declines with age, the mechanics of performance is everything and size counts most of all. What has been born is the Viagra generation, a generation relying on sexual stimulation aids to make up for the lack of spiritual energy and for the disconnection from our natural sexual intelligence. We have also become visually orientated, seeking out perfect archetypes to stimulate our sexual appetite, because of the barrage of pornographic and other-wise seductive images forced on us daily. Visual images, though sometimes pleasing, rob us of appreciation of true inner beauty, spiritual energy and the spiritual dimensions of our sexuality within relationship. They condition the mind and rewire our sexual intelligence into destructive patterning that overrides and suppresses sexual desire for our intimate partner. We are steered off the avenue of intimate sensual and energetic sexual experiences and onto a dead-end road of habitual sexual performance. The result is boredom and dis-enchantment with our sexual experiences. The conditioning of our minds and emotions can rob us of the joy of sex. It can push us instead into sexual cravings and addictions, leaving us hungering for enlightened lovemaking, a peak sexual experience with our Divine Complement. We may find it dif-ficult to reconcile the conflict between our conditioning and our soul's desire for sacred sexual union. We will have to bat-tle negative mind-sets and emotional wounds until spiritual truth and higher intelligence overcome them.

We share conscious and unconscious information with

our sexual partners. When that information is love, we are overjoyed by the good energy. However, sometimes we share corrupted information that is the product of our negative emotions and conditioning. I was counseling a woman recently who was suffering from a series of bladder infections. Her doctor diagnosed the problem as a bacterial invasion that was probably due to intimate sexual relations with her beloved. It made sense to her, as she and her partner enjoyed an active sex life. However, I could intuitively see that what was being transmitted though unconscious avenues were resentments and discordant energy. It was corrupting her sensitive sexual intelligence. She insisted that she and her partner loved each other very much. In fact, in the four years they had been together, they had never had an argument. I suspected her boyfriend was avoiding his real emotions, and so negative emotional currents were moving from him to her during sexual relations. This unconscious situation was compromising her immune system and manifesting as a low-grade infection.

The need to heal our sexual traumas, negative emotions and conditioned beliefs, which contaminate our innocence, becomes apparent to those of us who seek a more enlightened experience as sacred lovers. And the journey toward healing the wounds of sexual abuse may be a long one of building trust and emotional intimacy. We need time, compassion and the intelligence of love to heal the painful wounds, conditioned fears and corrupted attitudes that have harmed our sexual intelligence so that eventually we will feel free enough to surrender and enjoy the sexual exploration of our bodies. Innocence is our true state of sexual perfection. Our individual journey to reclaim sexual innocence is supported through our partnership with our beloved. The tenderness, time and attention they give us in intimate sexual experiences will help to heal from emotional wounds as well as the collective wounds of past generations that denied our sexual innocence.

Divine Principle:
The Bridal Chamber initiates us into the spiritual dimensions of sexual communion.

Our Divine Complement is our most compatible sexual partner. There is no one in the world or in any other dimension who can match us with the same volume of sexual creative harmony. No one else can bring us to the profound heights of spiritual ecstasy achievable through twin-soul sexual communion. Spiritual compatibility is determined by the design of two sets of harmonies that match and complement perfectly. Our twin soul's radiant rays represent a unique creative signature that complements our own individual signature, infusing us with beautiful energy and heightening our vibration. Through a language of light and a web of interconnectivity, communication and intelligence are shared and fusion is achieved. The combined or blended intelligence is creative and sexual, igniting spiritual passion and love. When we are awakened to the power of the twin lovers in the bridal chamber, our lovemaking will be infused with light.

To bring our twin lovers out of the ethers and down to earth requires that we bridge the intelligence of love with the intelligence of our sexuality. Heart center and sexual center must open, be cleansed and merge within our bodies to create a unified consciousness of pure and loving sexual energy.

Through intimate lovemaking that is heart-centered, tender, emotionally bonding and spiritually oriented, we create pathways of love for sexual healing and peak sexual experiences.

As spiritual practice and as partners, we can enter the chasm of our Stellar Hearts to touch the light of God within us. This light opens our hearts further and further with each intention we make to stay centered in our own hearts. We notice how the power of love infuses us with wellbeing and even joy and how it begins to create an open, safe and playful field of light that we can now share between us. This meditative preparation opens our hearts to each other and offers the greater potentials of God's love to enter our sexual experience. We share a higher volume of love's vibration with our partner when our individual channels of higher consciousness are opened and cleansed with God's light.

Within the bridal chamber our harmonies are already matched and intertwined in a divine dance to the melody of love, one orchestrated by the Creator. With surrender towards each other's hearts, we can experience a sharing of our harmonies matching in vibration, igniting our higher centers and raising our sexual intelligence to experience new peaks of pleasure and intimacy.

As we move again deeply inward, breaking through the stellar seal into the bridal chamber, we meet the magnificent vibrations of a profound sexual intelligence. We become aware of the radiant harmony of our stellar twin matching our own passionate fire, consciousness meeting consciousness. From within the bridal chamber, our minds can envision beautiful rays of color that represent each of our authentic signatures. The vibrant rays will be witnessed as two colors in combination drawn from a variety of color possibilities: gold, stellar blue, violet, crimson, pink or yellow. We bathe in our beloved's light, recognizing that our twin's creative intelligence is being shared with us in sacred communion, soul-to-soul and spirit-to-spirit. As the consciousness of our two hearts merge, light erupts and magnifies our experience even more. We are awakened to the cocreative harmony we always share in fields beyond this dimension. Now, however, through our conscious intention and awakened state, our spiritual sexual intelligence begins to create pathways into our bodies. We are initiated through the bridal chamber and bathed in each other's love and light, transcending the human condition and rising in recognition of our God/Goddess nature. As sacred lovers, we may begin enacting a lovemaking ritual in innocence, love and playful sexual expression. As with the hieros gamos ritual in which the initiate meets the divine through sexual communion, our purpose as divine lovers is to touch and realize God's consciousness in our hearts and God's power within our bodies. Together, we will travel over currents of light, plunge into immense waves of spiritual power and rise to spiritual ecstasy.

Chapter 8

The Highest Purpose

Divine Principle:
The co-creative harmony of Divine Complements unifies their consciousness to manifest their higher purpose together—their most important purpose is to co-create love.

"The purpose of a man is to love a woman and the purpose of a woman is love a man. Come on baby, start to play. Come on let's play, the game of love." These lyrics from a 1950s love song sum up the divine purpose of relationship—to love.

We are all looking for and trying to achieve "the Real Thing", a relationship that will fulfill our greatest hopes and desires for companionship and love, one that will be committed and lasting and will complete us inside and out. We also dream of a relationship through which we can spiritually grow to embrace God and the true meaning of life, beyond the mundane illusion that surrounds us every day.

To achieve 'The Real Thing' we must commit to a spiritual path of equality in relationship and pass through the narrow gate. That narrow gate represents humility, the kind of humility that forces us to fulfill each promise to love and cherish our twin even in the thick of adversity. Devotion and commitment will serve our individual spiritual advancement, as well as advance the relationship to higher ground. The higher ground of relationship is equality, divine consciousness and divine humanness, choosing love in every circumstance and therefore loving each other a little more each day. Our further commitment is to spread love outward to others and recognize that we are both lights in the world.

It can take considerable effort to experience and redevelop the level of love that was infused in us in the beginning. We must consciously enter our hearts to touch it every day and apply it to our interactions. We may have to fight to uphold it when the world or our own minds try to deny the truth of our hearts.

The effort and love we put into relationship may seem unrewarded at times. It's a lot like standing in front of a slot machine, dropping tokens into the slot and pulling the arm of a bandit that seems to eat up everything we put in. But if we continue to feed it, we might eventually hit the jackpot. Giving love to our partner day in and day out should result in a rewarding bounty that can sustain us if we are willing to hang in there long enough. The greatest bounty we will witness will be the spiritual growth of our partner, who through our gifts of love evolves to more love for themselves and appreciation for us.

The union of twin souls had a co-creative purpose to advance each soul through a conscious partnership, one that served each through intelligence, compassionate care, love and commitment. In the beginning, we promised never to take our Divine Complement for granted or take advantage of them. We asked ourselves to always consider what our partner needed to grow, often from our lead, and to always appreciate the invaluable lessons they in turn had to teach us. We may never attain the spiritual mastery in relationship that we'd aspired to, but we can become enlightened to love's power to heal us and move us into deeper intimate bonds that nurture our growth in increments.

The spiritual mastery we attain when we have balanced the male and female aspects of our higher selves propels us through life consciously creating and manifesting our dreams, desires and destiny. An intention to pursue our own design and aims must acknowledge the one who brings our picture into focus and who adds to the synergy to make it happen—our Divine Complement. "Stand by your man," a phrase most commonly seen as reflective of how things are achieved in a man's world, may have seemed valid in the 1950s, but it falls short of the mastery that equality can achieve. The evolved perspective demands equality in modern relationships, where partners team up to achieve the goals they envision. Behind the scenes a woman's love and creative power add more to her partner's success than most realize. His achievements are more theirs than his alone, even if he is the sole breadwinner. Through a mutual design and the energy she adds to his creative field, he may be lifted all the way up the corporate ladder or to wherever else he chooses to fulfill his goals.

Equality in relationship is the path that appreciates our individual wholeness, the equality of our masculine and feminine sides. Maintaining divine consciousness requires that we recognize and value our partner's reflection of the qualities and potentials that complete us. Our task is to embrace the equality of our partner and to let them take the lead at times when we need their insights to complement and add to our own.

Our Divine Complement's value to us will become evident as we collaborate to secure our future together. We will notice how easily we can manifest our hopes, dreams and goals through the co-creative design that ushers in a flurry of opportunities. The amount of creativity we can generate will depend on how in sync and harmonious we are with our mate. Neither of our wills should suppress the ideas, contribution and creative energy of the other, because if it does, the co-creative design is likely to fall apart. We will find that opportunities will not manifest as easily, and we will be forced to take stock of the situation and our failings before we can generate enough energy to put life back on course.

Recognizing that God is in every effort we make, whether or not we are consciously asking for God's help, is the ultimate realization. We are always free to use God's energy, regardless of what we choose to use it for. Our higher intelligence knows this constant and continuous communion with God. It knows that the spirit of God is radiating through us, under us and above us at all times. Through spiritual understanding of the Stellar Promise, we realize that our beloved Divine Complement is there, too, always adding to the equation.

At the spiritual dimension, the unified field of creative intelligence between Divine Complements reflects two spirits in action. As mentioned earlier, the communion of twin souls is represented as the number 44 in numerology. As spiritual mastery between two twin souls, it evokes the presence and harmony of God in communion, from within the template of our Stellar Heart. The trinity of harmony, created out of this union between twin souls and God, calls us to manifest our God/Goddess potentials and power on earth and to spread God's glory throughout the world. To achieve the Real Thing, we need to consciously add God to the equation of the relationship.

In this life, we have to work hard to consistently recognize God's presence in our lives, to cultivate God's power within us, and to love our partner and ourselves as God loves us.

I received a phone call from a dear friend of mine wishing me a merry Christmas. She was feeling disillusioned with her relationship, as the level of commitment was minimal, considering that they had been dating for almost a year. She told me that the big challenge seemed to be that her partner has no concept of God, no proof of God's existence in his life. He once asked her, "If there is a God, why is there so much suffering in the world?" Although she is not someone who chooses to worship God by going to church, the consciousness of God has always been in her heart, and she has been very much aware of God's miracles in her life. She said she became disillusioned after failing to help him understand God's presence and make him aware that the little miracles, which arrive when you least expect them, are evidence of God's power and presence.

The next evening, they went to a Prince concert with friends and had a wonderful time. Later, they went to a club, and she noticed that the sapphire in her ring was missing. She was devastated. The ring was a one-of-a-kind art-nouveau design from the 1930s and the stone was an unusual cut. Her roommate seemed confident that they would find the sapphire at the concert site. The next morning, they got up early and raced there to follow the hunch. She located the row of seats where they had been seated and combed the area. Suddenly, she saw the sapphire sitting on the seat of a chair in the row directly in front of where they had been sitting, as if an angel had placed it there. She hoped her boyfriend would recognize the magic of the ring's recovery as God's gift, but he dismissed it as a logical progression—by retracing her steps, she was bound to find it. He couldn't embrace the notion of a creative miracle, because he couldn't escape his logical mind, intuit the truth and put faith in a higher power. For my friend, it is a challenge to be in a relationship with someone who denies the existence of God and the miracles in life. Her job as a complement and friend is to steer him out of the prison of his logic and into the creative field where magic is everywhere. She must bring him into God's territory through her feminine wisdom, patience and grace. When he wakes up, she will be the proof of God's presence that he was unconsciously seeking.

The divine consciousness of God is a step beyond having faith in God. Others can instill faith in us that God exists, but eventually we will look for the proof through our own experience. Divine consciousness grows as we embrace the meaningful and magical experiences of life as proof of God's power to improve our life.

At the spiritual level, our connection with God is eternal. The same is true of the connection with our twin soul. We are forever bonded at the oversoul and in the template of love within our Stellar Heart, as we were in the beginning when God conceived us through his/her creative intelligence as stellar twins. This eternal commitment, the Stellar Promise, is a unity with God and our twin soul that can never be broken. As Divine Complements, our unique individual harmonies were sealed together as complementary rays that dance together always. Through lifetimes we have been parallel in evolution. While we may have been separated at times by circumstances and geography, we are always connected in our flight in the upper dimensions of consciousness, in a divine union of synergy that creates experiences for us on the playing field of life.

These experiences further us and further others whose lives we touch. As angels of light, we are God's messengers and servants, brought two by two into the world to offer each other and others around us a glimpse of God's most beautiful partnership.

Forever is a long time. We might wonder why, if these unions were intended to last forever, do couples fail at the lessons of love in any incarnation, such as the kind that would result in the death of the relationship? Doesn't "meant to be" mean that we can't miss? No, because fulfilling our destiny requires work and conscious choices of commitment. If the intelligence of love is lost to emotional neglect, mistreatment and disrespect, the creative path of relationship may dissolve. Failure occurs when one or both partners cannot rise enough to touch the divine within themselves or to see the divine in the other. These people cannot actualize the purpose of commitment to love in this life, because they have lost themselves and lost sight of the worth of their beloved. Many neglect the Stellar Promise in the same way they neglect God. They fail to see their partners' value in their lives. They lose faith in relationship like they lose faith in God because not every day is a miracle of love manifest before them. Some days can be full of hard lessons that test our compassion and understanding and push us to express love to fulfill our commitment to love. Before we can realize everlasting love, we have to be ready to love every day.

Even with the failure of the relationship in this life, the connection with our Divine Complement will continue in the upper dimensions and within the Stellar Heart. There is no way to remove it. It remains imprinted despite any misconception or denial of the union. Nothing changes it, just like nothing changes God's love. It is part of our motherboard.

Divine Principle:
The psychic connection between complements offers the gifts of
feminine intelligence to the consciousness of both.

Divine Complements are connected in many dimensions. Not only are we connected through the human bonds on this earthly plane and the upper planes or dimensions of the Divine, but we are also connected through psychic fields. The psychic realm is a realm of play where we dream together, tune in from time to time telepathically, and share psychic energy and information. Most every woman knows she can usually intuit her husband from a distance with a felt sense. If she is even more evolved, she may have clairvoyant images that spell out what he's really up to. She may know it when her spouse is cheating on her or when he is ill, before any diagnosis is made. She may know that he's going to show up at the door late, seeing him stuck in a traffic jam. If something more serious occurs, she may get a sinking feeling or a rush of fear at that very moment.

I met a woman recently who was in a long-distance relationship with her complement, whom she'd met online. He lived in Sweden and she in the U.S. They stayed in constant communication through e-mail and phone conversations until he could wrap up his commitments and move to the U.S. She said that she seems to have a sixth sense of when he is e-mailing her. One day, she had just broke for lunch and got an image in her mind of him at his computer. She went to her e-mail box, and there was an e-mail from him sent at the exact moment she had seen him in her mind's eye. She said that it's uncanny how psychic they both are and that she can't remember having that kind of connection with any of her previous partners.

Some couples are more psychically attuned to each other than others are. Some finish each other's sentences, something that is often frustrating to the communicator, or they can read each other's emotions with unprecedented accuracy. They are often in tune with each other's unexpressed needs. On a hunch, a husband may call his wife suggesting he bring home takeout for dinner, and it proves to be the perfect solution to her hurried day.

Some couples dream for each other, offering insight into problems and even forecasts of the future. A woman recently told me she dreamed that her husband was piloting an airplane and crash-landed. The plane was destroyed, but he walked away unscathed. The dream predicted a failed business venture that had barely gotten off the ground, a disappointment to both of them.

Some couples show up as partners in night dreams that they both recall in the morning, a phenomenon called mutual dreaming. Mutual dreams demonstrate how dreamers collaborate and create in the dream dimensions and participate in each other's imagery. They may help each other fly or fight each other's demons, co-creating wild adventures through which they learn about their co-creative field. They are usually surprised the next morning to hear each other report the same dream, scene by scene.

Couples can also be psychically bonded in ways that are not good for them. We all share energy in the psychic field, good energy as well as bad. It is common for partners to become too dependent on the others' radiant fields, consuming their psychic space and drawing from their spiritual power. These people are psychic vampires, stealing the harmony of their beloved, never aware that they are drawing from someone else's energy and not their own. It's as if they are seeking the light of God through their partners' radiant light rather than through their own higher selves. This depletes their partners of their vital life force, leaving them vulnerable to other influences that may on occasion penetrate their energy fields. It can even make them physically ill. It is usually so unconscious that they can't identify the problem without the help of an intuitive or a clairvoyant.

I was counseling a woman who was working on developing her inner strength and integrating aspects of her masculine side. Her spiritual guides had made a big issue of her need to develop spiritual strength and better psychic boundaries in her quest for wholeness. Her Divine Complement was a strong-willed man who had a great deal of psychic and spiritual power. As her complement, he reflected the inner strength and spiritual power of her repressed masculine side, and should she have internalized it, she would have been more balanced and integrated. She instead anchored herself straight into her husband's energy field, grounding herself in his power and using his harmony instead of her own. During a healing session, I recognized the problem when the image of her complement kept reappearing in her energy field. Quite often, people will unconsciously enter the field during a healing as they sense an opportunity for themselves. However, in her case, she was unconsciously calling him to her to stabilize her own energy. This kind of symbiotic relationship is unhealthy. The situation arises when people fail at integrating their own higher intelligence through the light of their higher selves. To be reliant on others' energy bodies will not help them develop their own.

Another client I saw regularly was a clairvoyant who was frequently challenged by others creeping into her energy field uninvited. Their souls seemed magnetized to her light, and she was unable to cope with the burden and drain on her energy. What was remarkable was that she couldn't perceive how she enabled them because of her unconscious wish to heal them. Nor was she aware of the fact that she often wandered into their fields, taking on their burdens and creating one big one for herself. With her husband, the issue became overwhelming and frustrating because of their close bond and lack of psychic boundaries. She was always jumping the fence of his psychic field to save him from inner demons. She would often complain that she was picking up his stress and his negative emotions. At one point he was experiencing a great deal of stress at work and she couldn't sleep a wink. He, on the other hand, slept like a baby because she was taking care of him so well at night. This kind of problem is common to couples who have strong emotional and psychic bonds. There are even those who will develop the same illness or physical conditions as their partners as a psychic sympathetic response. They may believe that they are helping them, but it seldom cures their partners' physical problems, because they need to learn their own lessons from the illness.

When couples primarily live in the physical and psychic dimensions, having not fully realized the dimensions of their light, there can be a great deal of confusion about whose energy is whose. "Am I you or are you me?" They identify too much with their partners' emotions, feeling their feelings and suffering with them. Boundaries are fuzzy, and the psychic field overwhelms them with negative emotions. The sharing of psychic energy can throw them off the course of integrating the potentials of their higher selves, and they find it difficult to evolve beyond emotional dependency. Their partners' Shadows and negative emotions may deny them satisfaction and freedom to experience their own emotions. They will find that they are sad or angry without cause. At some point, they will have to liberate themselves by addressing their needs as much as their partners'.

Evolution is bringing us all to a higher way of establishing and maintaining our energy. Through opening up to the potential of our higher selves, we are reactivating the matrix, which unifies our consciousness with the spiritual dimensions and with God. Through the creative intelligence of the higher self, our energy body becomes grounded in light. The radiant energy of our higher self creates a field of harmony that is stronger than what we could ever achieve with our psychic power. The field is like a boundary of light or a force field, protecting us from discordant or harmful negative energy. This field also shares information with others, giving light to all entering our space. At this level of integration, we are in communion with others rather than psychically dependent on them; this way of sharing energy is a stronger expression of the spiritual force because we feed others our light rather than consuming their discordant energy.

With our higher self integrated, we more readily share spiritual power with our Divine Complement by exchanging our radiant harmonies. This communion nurtures the spirit of the two of us and exchanges higher intelligence. There are numerous harmonies, codes of light and radiant color rays that the Creator gave us. These harmonies create a unique and elaborate matrix that is part of the individual's oversoul. The harmony of one complement impels its twin to higher states of consciousness, enabling their hearts to experience the harmony of God and opening them to new dimensions of consciousness. Some call this synergy simple attraction, believing it's only the biological sexual urge that's running them. However, this magnetic attraction is actually spiritual attraction. The sharing of spiritual energy pushes us to grow in intelligence. Sometimes this creates a cellular shift and healing that might be difficult to achieve on our own.

A year and a half ago, a good friend of mine was diagnosed with an aggressive form of cancer, B-cell lymphoma. She was living in Colorado at the time, having separated from her Divine Complement two years before. She was happy with her independent lifestyle, was nurturing herself and truly enjoying life when she was diagnosed with terminal cancer. In my assessment, the illness was caused less by her lifestyle and more by her relationship with a toxic parent whom she was symbiotically dependent on. Needless to say, she was clear that she needed a great amount of support from friends who loved and cared about her. She was firm that she wasn't going to go through with the medical model's recommendations. Her doctor had prescribed a series of chemotherapy treatments, which he advised she start right away, as there was no time to lose. She refused the treatments, intuiting that they could kill her, and chose instead to put her faith in God. She looked into her heart and was blessed with the wisdom of Jesus, who showed her she would be healed upon her return to Maui. I saw her the day she arrived but hardly recognized her. She had lost weight and the shadow of death seemed to permeate her energy field. She moved in with her ex-husband, who was anxious to do everything he could to care for her. Both she and her husband came to me for spiritual healing. I helped them to consciously use their spiritual energy by meditating together and exchanging their hearts' energy to unify their harmony. They learned to send the energy between their hearts in a figure eight, creating a healing communion. After six weeks, the lymphoma disappeared. Numerous CAT scans proved that there was no cancer in her body.

When her ex-husband found out she was ill, he was of

course worried and frightened. He realized that even though they were no longer husband and wife, their connection was still alive, strong and meaningful. He loved her very much. He supported her through the healing process but remained skeptical, as all logic and reason told him this was an incurable disease. He had watched his mother die of cancer. It was emotional torture to think that his beloved would die with as much pain and suffering. When she was miraculously cured, he learned firsthand of God's miracles. The miracle instilled in him faith in God's power and intervention, and he understood that his recommitment to her was part of the equation. Their creative harmony created a field of intelligence with God that altered their lives. It saved her life and pulled them back into service to the love they had left behind four years before. Each of them was to learn an important lesson from this miracle, the most important one being that their divine purpose together had not been completed. The crisis brought them back together to grow more fully into the intelligence of love, to share compassion and healing power, and to honor and appreciate their union as an expression of God—a union that could create more miracles for them.

The bonds of the human dimension can offer as much healing. Through compassion, love and understanding, we may offer emotional healing to our beloved in ways that psychotherapy cannot. We will intuitively sense symptoms of depression, grief or resentment before they are communicated. We will wish to lessen their pain and help them identify the source. Wounds from early neglect, loss or abuse will surface, usually when someone is ready to address them. The insights we offer at those critical times may pinpoint and illuminate painful events and help our partner begin to let go and forgive. Emotional intimacy is a bonding and healing agent at the human level of relationship. The choice to stand as a compassionate witness, always maintaining an emotional connection and the intelligence of love, will nurture our partner through any emotional storm.

Some Divine Complements will discover that they share a parallel childhood horror story of emotional or physical abuse. They will mirror to each other the wounds of their similar histories. A mother who was neglectful, a father who yelled, a brother who was jealous—all will be illuminated, along with the emotional pain each had to endure. In this way, a couple gains insights into their personal wounds and can begin to heal their pain and feed their hunger for love.

Couples may find that their histories are stories with the same plot, only with different characters playing the villains or heroes. For some, the stories will unravel as amazing chronologies of similar events that they will both have to muddle through. A couple may discover that they are wounded healers confronting two dark histories at once. Love will be the ingredient needed to heal the deepest wounds. Relationship is meant to nourish and nurture the divine child and playmate as much as the sacred lovers.

In relationship, childhood wounds are often the first needing attention, because they can surface suddenly when our emotions are triggered. The negative emotions, attitudes and beliefs associated with these wounds will have to be cleansed so that they are not projected onto the relationship. Blame and emotional outbursts damage trust. *What we desire and need from our partner in the way of emotional support and sensitive communication is what we will also have to give.* Listening and responding to our partner with an open heart and love's intelligence will open the door for compassionate sharing. Not only will the things we do and the time we take to address the emotional turbulence bring about healing, but something will be translated to our partner through the harmony in our heart. Information is shared like it is between two computers that have been networked together. Within invisible dimensions, a higher intelligence of love will be communicated, absorbed and synthesized, with the potential of healing us at the core.

Our life path is co-created every day, harmonized perfectly to help us evolve through lessons of love. Side by side with our complement, our experiences test our love so that we will begin to stand on a firmer foundation of respect and commitment. Our goals will be co-created and manifest through the synergy of the complementary harmony with our partner. If there is something to work out, there will be no escaping each other. The creative force behind our mutual design will always put us onto the path of the other, even when we wish to go it alone.

I remember an occasion when my complement and I were teaching a workshop and needed to communicate before the course began. We were traveling separately because he wanted time for himself before the session. He said he needed the space to think, but I sensed his design was not to include my input. I conceded and rode with one of my students. We stopped at Safeway to buy refreshments for the group on the way. There were about 10 stores we could have stopped at, but our choice was co-created to bring my complement and me face to face. As we pulled into the parking lot, there he was getting out of his car. There was obviously no escape from the communication that needed to occur. And I wasn't going to let the opportunity for the two of us to clear the air and to set the day's schedule slip away. I told him I thought it was obvious that we were meant to collaborate more and insisted that I ride with him so that we could discuss the day's activities. These magical kinds of encounters, facilitated by divine intervention and divine timing, are sparked by the creative intelligence of two who harmonize to make things happen that are in the interest of higher good. They will be created through a design that makes the world seem magically perfect or confrontational and challenging, depending on how we interpret them. A higher intelligence is in charge of creating the playing field for tests of love and higher understanding. We need only to evolve to learn the rules for mastering our relationship through joining in honest communication every time we are pushed into each other's arms.

The creative field of relationship will make everything happen. The dreams we envision with our complement will become manifest only through our conscious will to stand as equals, contributing and collaborating on the physical plane. In the spiritual dimensions, our souls' intentions set the course. Our thoughts and intentions contribute to the spiritual field of creativity. Fulfillment will be realized when our souls and our conscious intentions move in the same direction. We can learn to soar on a trail of love, magically manifesting opportunity through conscious intention, and share with our partners the fruits of this collaboration. On the other hand, we can choose to act selfishly, denying our complements credit for their contributions and plummet into disgrace.

I had a couple of friends who, as Divine Complements, had a creative destiny and purpose to produce enlightening films. They met, fell in love and soon realized they had complementary talents that could be combined to fulfill their divine purpose. The man had already produced several documentaries. The woman had been groomed in Los Angeles as an actress. She had only had a couple of bit parts but had enough knowledge of the industry to recognize worthy material. When they came together, it was as if a power grid had been turned on. The woman had a strong commitment to producing films with a spiritual message. She offered her partner spiritual insight, aligning him with a higher understanding of the kind of film that could contribute a positive message to humanity. She was the voice of inspiration, and she held her vision tight to her chest. She also was a magnetic and energetic force who could attract writers offering scripts in the genre of film she had envisioned. The creative harmony they produced together created an explosion of opportunities for them. Scripts flooded through the door. With her partner's production background, talents and relentless drive, they were a "match made in heaven" destined to spread a powerful message to the world. However, they fought for recognition of their talents not from the world but from each other. The man, who was the achiever, thought he could forge his way without honoring the talents of his complement and complimenting her efforts. They couldn't give each other credit for what they'd achieved. They fought for equality and recognition of their worth. Their egos clashed, and the relationship soon ended. I was sure I could hear the angels in heaven cry when they parted.

Divine Principle:
Supporting the growth of our partners on their quest toward Divine Humanness will reward us with good karma. Our transgressions against others will result in bad karma that affects us both.

Complementary relationship carries with it the responsibility for each other's progress on the road to divine humanness. We offer each other safeguards to ensure that in the creation of our lives together, we are responsible to each other and accountable for our own mistakes, match each other's integrity, and have respect not only for each other but also for everyone else. We depend on our partners to guide us to the right decision in life and to point out our mistakes even when we think we have mastered it all. At other times, we will just admire and follow their example. And in some senses, our failures will be their failures. Through their achievements and as result of their earnest efforts, we will reap and appreciate the rewards that arrive at the front door. Should our values fail to measure up as conscious choices that consider the welfare not only of our own family but the family of the human race, there could be negative repercussions. Engaging in business practices that lack integrity and regard for human life is a common failing that many partners tolerate. Some vow not to stick their noses into their partner's business affairs, ignoring any disregard for integrity, especially when it feeds, clothes and cushions the family. A vow of silence represents collusion under the divine human code of ethics. It is our karmic responsibility to enlighten our partner to what we believe is right or wrong, especially when we know they are wrong.

If our partner commits a crime against society and is punished for it, we may suffer the consequences also, especially if they face prison time and bring shame to our name. When it comes to finances, we may not think it's much of a crime if our partner won't pay child support for children from a previous marriage. Their responsibility and accountability to those children is obvious, but what may not be so obvious is our role to make sure they are fulfilling their karmic promises. The complementary path demands that we help our partner become accountable and responsible for karmic debts and promises, even if they were made before we came along. We may very well have to pull out our own checkbook to make good our partner's karmic promises.

Even the most honest complement may make a mistake in judgment. George Burns told a not-so-funny story about the time he bought a diamond bracelet for Gracie from a man he and Jack Benny considered a friend. Jack had also bought a comparable piece of jewelry for his wife, Mary, from him. George thought the bracelet would light up Gracie's eyes when he surprised her with it that evening. It did. What happened next was an even bigger surprise. Their friend's maid knew something that George didn't know: The jewelry had been smuggled. In anger, she had turned her boss in to the authorities. As a result, George and Jack were both arrested and convicted of receiving smuggled property. This embarrassment cost both George and Gracie thousands in fines and attorney's fees. At the end of the ordeal, they got the bracelet back, but Gracie immediately gave it away, probably because she thought it had already cost them too much. Whether or not George knew more than he was willing to admit, this twist of fate must have humbled him in front of Gracie.

Karma from our failures in previous lifetimes can result in the kind of situations that George found himself in. Periods of extreme hardship may represent a karmic payback intended to teach us to value others, not how much money we have in our bank accounts. Our lessons will become our family's endurance tests. As Divine Complements, we agreed to help each other complete the karmic lessons brought forward into this life, including those that may require us to sacrifice something or tolerate limitations. Financial hardship, health issues or other trying circumstances will put love to the test. We will always have to summon our love and understand that love will help us ride the tail of karma over bumps and around treacherous curves.

Karmic laws are in effect for us as long as we are members of the human race. Transgressions against our neighbors or family will have consequences for us as well as for our partner. If we are fighting with the next-door neighbor over the property line, we may find that our partner will be pulled into the dispute even though he or she doesn't care that the neighbors' rosebush is planted a foot onto our property. They may in fact think it looks beautiful. If they're doing their job, they may give us a bit of wisdom to chew on, such as the notion that disputes can be best-settled with openhearted communication. If we are failing as a parent by neglecting our promises, our partner may have to call it to our attention and expect that we change direction and drive to the baseball diamond or the soccer field to catch our child's next game. Our complement is our life coach, guiding, encouraging and bringing us to the glory of divine humanness.

Divine Principle:
Divine complementary relationship can enlighten us to the meaning and magic of life.

The more our consciousness opens to the creative spiritual dimension, the more we will see that the world and our life together are but a dream. It is a "dream reality"—meaning that it is synergistically created at levels that are normally invisible to our eye but can be seen through the lens of our hearts. These dimensions are not above us but interwoven within the world we already know. Our creative potentials are at work in a creative field that produces experiences through which we learn universal principles that advance and reward us. When we are clear in our hearts and awakened to the spiritual power behind our complementary partnership, the synergy between us is stronger. God's grace follows us everywhere. Anything we can imagine can manifest, especially if it is for our highest good and for the good of those around us.

At times, we will find that we are in-sync, dancing through the dimension of the creative field manifesting everything our hearts desire. These will be times of good fortune and success. The banquet will be set before us, and we will feast on life's offerings. At such times, we are in the flow and following the currents of creative harmony that were set in motion by our thoughts, prayers and intentions. Every day will be perceived as full of miracles of grace and meaningful experiences. We will be magically rewarded every time we put effort and insight to work within the relationship, helping our partner awaken to these dimensions and evolve next to us. The stronger the love, the better able our spirit's creative force will be to fulfill the dreams we envision together. We might even notice that mountains of limitations crumble and fall before our eyes. Nothing seems insurmountable when two are creatively dreaming a result with the magic of love.

In the playing field of dream reality, signs will be offered as guideposts, pointing the way to the fulfillment of our dreams. Synchronistic signs will spring into view just when we need a little information. We will need our feminine intuition to translate these signs into meaningful answers. Whether it is a symbol on someone's T-shirt, a message spelled out on a license plate, a bumper sticker, or a formation in the clouds, it will nudge us to notice it and ponder the meaning. A diving logo repeatedly appearing on T-shirts worn by passersby may signal the need to dive into our emotions to discover what we are hiding from our partner or ourselves. A little boy practicing riding his bike in front of the driveway at the very moment we wonder why our spouse is late in coming home may mean that they are out practicing some independent action that needs some effort to master or that they are just out having some fun. I love to watch for the clues and messages of dream reality, following the thread of messages strung about God's dimension. When I see two doves bowing and cooing on the front lawn, as if they are worshiping each other, I recognize them as the lovers and divine messengers telling me it's time to resume writing this book. When the wind chimes ring in the distance, it affirms that I have written something meaningfully inspiring at that very moment.

By beginning to interpret life as a dream that is full of meaningful messages, warnings and information, we become enlightened to a hidden dimension. This dimension has always been there—we just needed to enter a state of divine consciousness to perceive it. In dream reality, we are lifted into a free zone called "no time." It becomes imperative that we understand and stand within the moment. We recognize that our previous concept of time within a fixed third-dimensional view offers us little spiritual interaction and meaning. But when we let go of this illusion, suddenly the world is magical and is communicating its meaningful messages at every turn. Everything gets our attention. A bird singing in the distance, a child crying next door, a car honking on the street may be punctuating our thoughts in the moment. We recognize our connection to everyone and every experience as momentous. We are enlightened to magic erupting everywhere we look, and we begin to expect a miracle around every corner. Expectation lights the dimension. We master the dimension when we correctly interpret the serendipity, synchronicity and hidden messages in the world each time we notice them.

The dance through dream reality with our beloved can offer guidance and clarity about the decisions we make on a daily basis. The dream reality may even offer us a little humor. For instance, if we wish to interrupt our beloved's afternoon of playing golf with a petty problem, we may be startled at the very moment we pick up the phone by the sound of screeching tires in the distance asking us to stop, think and chill out. We may be warned when we are creating adversity that might get in the way of our commitment to the intelligence of love. The more serious the infraction against love's intelligence, the more blatant the reverberation of signs. Love's intelligence echoes intelligent signs in the world around us.

If the signs from our higher self are not obvious to us, we may need a stronger warning to get the picture. Our partner may be the one to warn us that things are moving in the wrong direction. A woman I talked with recently had been frustrated with a recent change in her husband's behavior. He started going out for drinks with friends from work almost every night. He had never seriously cultivated friendships before, so at first she thought it was fine if he went out with his buddies if it made him happy. When the evenings out became longer and longer and he started coming home at 2 a.m., she knew she would have to draw a loving line. She had a long conversation with him, letting him know that she interpreted his staying out till the wee hours of the morning as neglect of his responsibility to her and their children. She added that there would be consequences and casualties if the behavior continued. What she meant was that she would leave him for the sake of her happiness and self-respect. He got part of the picture and curtailed his nights out. A couple of months later, the creative design of this lesson provided him with the rest of the picture and proof that she was right.

The friend he hung out with most on his evenings out was thrown out on his ear because of his continued neglect of his wife. The final episode in the creative collaboration among friends and lovers had offered a dramatic ending, proving that there are painful consequences to the neglect of relationship.

Divine Principle:

God is with us always.

Divine Complements get an increasingly clear picture of something deeply meaningful: their connection to God. As couples grow more closely bonded through the intelligence of love, it will become obvious that they are not alone. God has always been a directing force in a mutual dream, offering grace when we've needed it, guidance when our own insights have not been sufficient, and visible signs of God's subtle presence on Earth. "The One Intelligent One" is unifying twin souls through his/her love 24 hours a day. Twin souls and God create three, the most sacred trinity—the power of God realized and manifest through sacred relationship. Acknowledging and understanding the three-part harmony will empower us to reach love's crescendo daily.

Our souls always summon us to recognize that God is at the center of our existence, above, below and everywhere in between. God's love is the miracle two can rely on. A reliance on God will take us further than we can get if we try to create our lives all by ourselves. Without God's grace, we may still achieve our dreams, visions and goals, but they may prove less meaningful or even empty. We may blindly believe we are at the center of it all, just like the bumper sticker that says, "It's all about me," until we realize "me" isn't enough. We will then seek a higher power to illuminate the greater meaning of life.

God supports our progress and achievements in becoming divinely human. Divine Humanness is the greatest achievement for each human soul in that it manifests God's love through conscious choice and action in everyday life. It means fulfilling our promises to give love, to be compassionate, to bless the world with the grace of our service, and to give care and attention to those closest to us. We can meditate all day, pray all night, go to church on Sunday, temple on Friday, visit 100 sacred sites, hang a rosary on our rearview mirror and still not get the honor we are after from God if we abandon our commitment to our complement or our children.

Some spiritual seekers conceptualize the pathway to the realization of the Absolute as a solitary journey. Enlightenment is seen as being reached through prayer, contemplation and meditation, renouncing the world and everyone in it for a time in order to break through the veil of the grand illusion of separation. Such spiritual disciplines too often see relationship as getting in the way of climbing the mountain to God, considering celibacy and a monastic life the only way to prove devotion and obtain the keys to heaven.

Buddha himself abandoned his wife and child in his quest for higher truth and liberation from what he termed the bondage of human relationship. Of his son, who was born just before he left on what was to be his seven-year quest for enlightenment, he said, "A fetter (*rahula*) has been born, a bondage has been born." This is how his son Rahula was named. Although Buddha pierced through the veil into the higher mind and cosmic consciousness and undoubtedly became enlightened, he perhaps did not understand the bond that no effort could break: God's Stellar Promise, the unification and constant communion with his Divine Complement. He obviously proved himself divinely human and a world redeemer by spreading his wisdom and teachings, but I can't help thinking he accumulated some bad karma for abandoning his son and his wife.

Achieving enlightened states of self-realization, cosmic consciousness or nirvana may end our suffering for a time, bring us to peace and blissful states, but we may still fall short of personal redemption. Enlightened masters must return with the elixir of wisdom and enlighten others. Through spiritual practice, they have made a conscious connection with their higher selves' potentials to transcend this reality and experience the core light within themselves. It expands them beyond their own ego identities into cosmic consciousness or at-one-ness, revealing that there is no separation between mind and matter. They realize that we are pure consciousness, an in-breath and out-breath of some indefinable source.

However, this experience represents something like fool's gold, as it alone will not transfigure material reality or end duality within the soul. Nor will it automatically prove us worthy of the next step: absolution. One remains separated until ready to recognize the worth of God, the Absolute, as being supreme to the self. Some will mistakenly think they have touched the Absolute Godhead, during enlightened states. Others will return from such experiences convinced that there is no God, only the "I am presence" or god self through which they transcended the human dimension to become "one with the cosmos" or "one with the universe." Perhaps it is because the light empowers them and deceives them at the same time. They have awakened to God's power within themselves and integrated the higher mind, but the ego becomes identified with the God self and loses perspective and respect for the Absolute Godhead. They fail to recognize that they never got all the way home, that they have not been absolved of the karma that still separates them. They may feel good after having dismembered their ego, shed the cloaks of illusion and risen to the heights of cosmic bliss, but they often return in service to their ego. Those who remain enlightened, however, choose humility and service as the path of further redemption. They dutifully teach the path that enlightened them. They indeed are pure of heart, bringing their devotees as far as they have gone themselves.

This is still not Christ consciousness, however. Jesus enlightened us all to what it takes to enter the kingdom of God: love, forgiveness, absolution by God, commitment to honor God and service to love. No world redeemer—no Buddha, Gandhi or Mother Teresa—can end the duality of the world through consciousness-raising or even through compassion. It will arrive as Jesus said, when God decides the moment is right.

Christian ideology offers another half-truth path for those who seek God's glory. Christianity as a religion teaches us that if we put our faith in God and Jesus Christ, all our problems will be solved. Redemption is seen as having come through the Crucifixion and Resurrection of Jesus Christ, our savior, not through individual redemption. God is personified as a patriarchal ruler who is just and sometimes punishing. Adhering to God's laws is the way to fight the power of evil in one's life. God and Satan, although on opposing teams, are outsiders looking in, manipulating the life of the serious Christian. The path of righteousness represents a moral Christian life, obeying God's laws. Presumably, this path will bring one the glory of God's honor, opening the gates to the Kingdom of Heaven.

Unification with God can be achieved only through death or through God's salvation at the ending time.

Whether at-oneness and righteousness can live on the same block is questionable, as one seeks God through the interior life while the other seeks God through the exterior. One path can lead to enlightenment now, the other only in the afterlife. Both paths lost sight of the complementary truth in the other, in much the same way that Divine Complements often ignore the balance offered in each other's reflection. Each path holds a significant piece of the truth, if not half of it. The reason for this split in spiritual philosophy between East and West is the same reason that twin complements battle each other for equality in a marriage. The split-soul imprint split our view of God as well as our view of how to get to God. The masculine faces outward, away from the beloved feminine, and the feminine faces into her own heart, ignoring the masculine. Eastern spiritual doctrines reflect a more feminine perspective. The journey to God moves inward through the labyrinth of the soul to the point of light at its center. It relies on inner silence, intuition and clear sight, casting out the masculine mind in favor of the feminine inner sanctum. On the other hand, Western religion views the journey to God as a conscious, willful and righteous battle to defeat the forces of evil. It glorifies God as masculine intelligence, and its seekers are rewarded with glory for following the path of the Son of God, also personified as masculine.

The inner marriage puts an end to this separation in spiritual views. God is in everything, above and below, and is supreme and glorified. The quest for God is both an inner journey and an outer one. God's consciousness can be touched by surrendering the ego through meditation and by opening and entering the center of the heart. There we can achieve self-realization of our unified God/Goddess intelligence and experience cosmic consciousness. Karma will always have to be completed through conscious interactions in the outer life. We must demonstrate acts of love that make up for the times we chose hatred. Karmic debts can also be forgiven and absolved by God as a result of prayer so that their weight no longer limits our experiences. Karma cannot be burned off through the purification of touching the light in meditation. There is one God supreme who must be honored as offering us individual salvation as well as salvation to the world. It is unlikely that salvation will be achieved in any other way. It is through God's love and forgiveness that we will all come home, ending the separation that denied us God's perfection. However, through death of the weaker aspects of our personalities and rebirth into higher states of consciousness we may experience an afterlife within this life. We can be reborn divinely human.

The path of Divine Humanness demands that we travel a road lit by God's light. Our daily interactions demand that we become God-like, choosing love over all other thoughts and intentions. Forgiveness is one of the most important spiritual principles we will have to master on the path to Divine Humanness. Forgiveness brings about an end to the hatred that exists between two when betrayal has caused separation in their hearts. In much the same way that forgiveness denies evil its power, forgiveness in relationship frees us from the pain of further separation and distancing. Our heart is our own Kingdom of God to which we are welcomed every day we enter it. When we forgive, we put out a welcome mat for our beloved's return to our good graces. Our forgiveness will earn us a measure of God's grace. We will be freed from our resentments and be free to love our partner again.

Help for our relationship can be a prayer away. Prayer is

a way of extending ourselves to God, honoring God's role in our life. Prayer may provide the very answers and intervention we need, especially during difficult times in our relationship. Praying together is a ritual that few couples practice together. Many see prayer as something we do alone, in silence, or in church, where our words are not ours alone.

I fondly remember, as a child, watching my grandmother say her prayers every night, morning, afternoon and sometimes all through the day, depending how much she wanted from God. On her home altar she had a picture of her departed son, whom she grieved her entire life, along with pictures of Mother Mary and Jesus. The frankincense was as thick as her suffering. I don't know what she prayed for, because her prayers, read from a prayer book, were chanted in Greek. Whatever her prayers were, I don't think God appreciated them much, as nothing seemed to change in our family. If anyone had asked for my input, I would have prayed for my mother to lose her job so she could spend more time with me. As a matter of fact, I think my grandmother did pray for my mother's job security, as it was what kept her supplied with new hats from I Magnin. So maybe God *was* listening. Needless to say, my grandmother didn't recognize that I may have been the answer to her prayers all along, filling the empty spot in her heart left by the loss of her son. In looking back, I think she should have included my mother and me in prayer time. Something more magical and meaningful might have occurred each time she lit the candle on the altar. We may have grown to love's intelligence together and gotten along much better.

Prayer creates communion with God and opens our hearts to enjoyment of the God connection. The transmitter and receiver of our heart must be turned on to embrace God's miracles, and our voice must be loud enough for God to understand what we are asking for. The communion of prayer with our beloved in the presence of God can be a humbling exchange. Two hearts linked with the Creator creates the three-part harmony that brings grace through the door. By entering our individual hearts, we make conscious contact with God. The prayers we say together are 10 times as loud as those we say alone.

I had a God moment in the grocery aisle just a while ago with a woman who had something to share about prayer. I had run into her in three stores at the local mall. At last I mustered up the courage to say, "I think we are running into each other for a divine purpose." She told me she and her husband had been married for 59 years and vacationed on the islands each year. Unsolicited, she spoke on the nature of prayer. She told me that as a Christian Scientist, she was a firm believer in the power of prayer. But she added that most people mumble their prayers as if they are ashamed to ask God for anything. She said, "You have to go to your heart and ask God with all the power and authority you have, forgive, be humble and sincere." She also shared that she had prayed for a long time that her husband would open his eyes to God. Finally, after years of praying that he would join her in going to church, he opened his eyes to something wonderful that was obviously happening to her every Sunday. She always came through the front door beaming with joy. He finally started going to church with her to see what the hoopla was all about. My sense was that her radiant heart was more his altar than the one at church.

Setting up a prayer ritual requires the surrendering of some time to honor God's presence in our lives. Once we enter our Stellar Heart, we are connected individually with God and are ready to call our beloved into the communion at our heart's altar. A simple "bless you, my beloved" will send our beloved the harmony of love, and a reciprocal "bless you" will tie the knot. Tuning the instrument of the heart to create the three-part harmony sends our intention on a stream to be caught by the heart of the Creator. We may ask for a lot or just a little to support us in getting our dreams off the ground. What we ask for should naturally support the bonds of the relationship. A standard prayer tag line such as " if it is in our highest interest or for our highest good" may guarantee an outcome that supports us best; we trust God to know what is for our highest good. We in turn must be ready to let go of desires that go against the grain of our soul's purpose. If we truly welcome God's creative plan for us, we may pray that God helps put into place a creative field of what will best fulfill our divine purpose.

The harmony of prayer is a humbling experience of communion with God that opens us further to the creative purpose of love that three share. The harmony will fill our bodies with healing power, grace our lives with light, and manifest our creative destiny.

Divine Principle:

A co-creative destiny of service may be the avenue through which Divine Complements serve humanity. Our promise is to fulfill it together through the intelligence of love and mutual respect for each other's talents and contributions.

Complements often have a perfect synergistic plan and design to achieve a combined destiny that serves others. They may be authors who write a book together. They may work in

TV or radio broadcasting, fulfilling a promise to inspire the mainstream. Or they may have political aims to serve humanity. Both may wake up to this destiny together, or each may have envisioned a part of it long before they met. Each complement comes with the right ingredients and talents to contribute to their meaningful purpose. However, they may have to sort through some baggage of inequality in order to put it all together and be satisfied with the results.

Two of my students are complements who came together after their first marriages were long over and the children were grown. It became clear that they had a spiritual mission together, as both were committed to a similar vision of teaching consciousness and spirituality in the Los Angeles area. When I met them, the woman, a psychotherapist and yoga teacher, had already stepped onto the path of teaching groups. She had put together a successful private practice integrating spirituality and psychotherapy. She was devoted to her beloved and eager for him to join her vision but also concerned that they might not be able to make it financially if he stopped working to pursue his piece of the vision. During the first years, he supported them with proceeds from the sale of his house and with a home-repair business while she pursued her private practice and teaching seminars. His job was taking a toll on his health, and it became clear that his path as a spiritual teacher was waiting for him. He held a vision of teaching with her as well as producing a television show aimed at raising the consciousness of others. He was at the stage in his spiritual development of rising to his authentic purpose, while she was already down the path. About two years ago, he put a consciousness-raising public-access television show together, featuring guests whom he interviewed on a variety of topics. The talk show, which relies on public donations, is now a success. His wife went back to work at a mental health agency to better support them when finances became lean. They had reversed roles to learn about equality in relationship and achieve a karmic balance. Both needed to humble themselves through the intelligence of love to know that, if they were to stand alongside as equals, each needed to support the growth and vision of the other for a time. The balance, love and harmony of their relationship was the avenue through which they could achieve their spiritual mission. With love, respect for each other's talents, commitment to the future and the grace of God, they are evolving and contributing to their community through a unified presence.

One complement's special talents may reflect the hidden talents of the other. They need to rise in unison to a place of equality for their mission together to be accomplished. It is often the case that one has gained more recognition than the other even though their talents are equal, and their task will be to learn from each other, strive for equality and develop mutual respect.

We can look back at the examples set by the comedy teams of George Burns and Gracie Allen and Lucille Ball and Desi Arnaz, to see how some couples succeed and some fail in their commitment to love when they have divine destinies together. George said he always had to lead the way and encourage Gracie's abilities. With each transition—from Vaudeville to radio to the movies and finally to television—he had to nudge her along. He played to her sentiment that if he was happy, she would be happy. He said she could never deny him what he wanted. She felt too guilty because his vision of their mission was too strong.

As for Lucy and Desi, God's arms were wrapped around them as they co-created their destiny together. The three-part harmony brought about abundant opportunity to perform the miracle of divine complementary comedy on television. We learned to laugh and appreciate how opposites can complement so well, and how women could rise to equality with men. Although their achievement and contribution remain in our hearts, their love for each other could not weather the storms that neglect of the relationship caused. Once the love was gone and they divorced, the empire they had built together toppled.

We have few examples of husband-and-wife partnerships in the public eye anymore. If such love matches do happen, they dissolve quickly. My thoughts are that in the collective field, the King and Queen, who sought to serve humanity, have been dethroned and separated by a culture that wishes to deny maturity. It seeks to remain forever in adolescence, rekindling romantic notions about love to satisfy an insatiable hunger for the Real Thing. However, the Real Thing is something we have to deem as worth the effort and worth respecting. It must be guided by maturity and strengthened through the bonds of faithful commitment. Kings and Queens can't rise when the lovers aren't energized and faithful to their vision. All four archetypes are likely to fall from grace, and humanity will not be served their bounty.

Chapter 9

Second Chance

Divine Principle:
We reset the reunion time of our divine destiny each time we need to clear the path of the obstacles to love. Divine timing is nothing we wait for; it is what we live for.

Divine timing is a concept most imagine as a cosmic zone beyond this dimension, set by the unseeable, perhaps God, and springing up in the moment we least expect it. It is eagerly awaited and imagined. When it arrives, it ushers in all the magical experiences that fulfill our deepest wishes. It hails from the dimension of somewhere over the rainbow, a place like Oz, where the unexpected can materialize.

227

The Greeks credited Chronos, the father of days, or Father Time, with having set the order of real time in the third dimension. According to Greek mythology, he was the first-born god and is said to exist in the fourth dimension. Under Chronos' time, life is ordered, rhythmic, and predictable.

In perceiving our reality, we naturally depend on the concept of time to guide us out of the past, through the present and into the future. Without it, we have no reference point for measuring the human experience of cause and effect. We might imagine that we would be utterly confused and in chaos without it. However, in the dimensions of our hearts and the creative intelligence of our oversoul, time ceases, and we experience a consciousness of love that is external and in the moment. This zone is where stellar twins exist and where they co-create the magical experience of their earthly reunion as well as the course of their destiny.

While we are under the thumb of Chronos and locked into time's measured increments—hours, days, weeks, months and years of our lives waiting for fulfillment—we appear to be uninvolved in the creative design of the future and often lose patience with life's course. For those waiting for their Divine Complement, the waiting may seem like an eternity. A woman may worry that her biological clock will run out before her beloved meanders through the door ready for the altar. Or a man may fear that he will lose his sex appeal before the woman of his dreams recovers from her last relationship. Life goes on and, for some time, seems to pass them by. However, there is a time when everything comes together to create the magical moment for the commitment to love to begin.

Who sets the clock of divine timing? We do, through our co-creative harmony, in another dimension of our experience with our complement. Divine timing is created out of the synergy between our higher selves, who come together free of the thumb of Chronos after we've measured our progress in terms of evolution, matching it against our initial karmic plan for reunion and co-creating the creative miracle of the right moment. This can happen at any age, 5 or 75, depending on each soul's progress in fulfilling the milestones of its destiny plan. Whenever it happens, most complements agree, it was the perfect moment in time.

I met a beautiful elderly twin-soul couple, Ellen and Bill, at Borders Books one afternoon and walked up to them thinking they might have a story to offer about the long-term commitment of divine complementary relationship. I commented that they were a beautiful couple who looked like they had been together forever. The 83-year-old woman replied, "No, we've only been married for eight years." She and her husband, 82, had met in church after both had lost their lifelong mates to cancer within months of each other. She told me she had never been introduced to Bill, but one Sunday she saw him winking at her from the other side of the sanctuary. She decided to invite him out for coffee, "to set him straight" that she was not interested in a romantic relationship. It was not her wish to have another man in her life, but she did tell me she had prayed to God to end her loneliness. Bill interjected that it was by "divine design" that his beloved came into his life at the right moment.

Ellen said she had grown a lot through her first marriage, to a man she considered to be a good man but very different from Bill. Nursing him through his long illness had proved tiring, however. She admitted she had outgrown the need to be a caregiver, always putting others before herself, and had vowed that she was ready to begin thinking about herself. Bill said the care she gives him is what he appreciates most about her, along with her sincerity and honesty. The commonality of losing their life mates to cancer seemed to have been a meaningful parallel lesson for these soul mates, who came together very late in life for a second chance at love. Their reunion in this life came late to accommodate each other's personal karmic promises. Through my clairvoyance, I saw that Bill had had significant karma to complete with his first wife. Ellen's soul had compromised and joined him when his soul's lesson was complete. It proved a beautiful divine design that further demonstrated that divine timing for a soul-mate reunion can happen at any age.

They laughingly told me they kept their romance a secret from their friends at church until they were ready to announce their plans to get married. In trying to set the date for the wedding, they drew straws, asking whether they should get married immediately, in six months, or at another date they would agree on later. They drew the shortest straw, meaning that they were to marry right away. The day they planned to announce to the congregation their engagement, the pastor's sermon was titled "Divine Design." a meaningful synchronicity for Bill who referred to their relationship as having come together by divine design. Bill said he had to chuckle, knowing that God had his hand in making their engagement announcement a meaningful and inspiring day for everyone in the congregation.

Waiting for happiness and fulfillment can send some into desperation, leaving them unable to recognize that their mind-sets and beliefs slow the hands of time. I recently met a woman in her late forties who felt defeated because she could not find an equal partner. She had every rationalization in the book to explain why it hadn't happened yet, including her observation that Afro-American men were not choosing women of color where she lived. She was angry, lonely and disillusioned. In my intuitive reading, I could see that she had

had a karmic relationship about four years before, and I asked her about it. She told me she had dated a married man and felt terrible about the whole experience. She had been left with a negative attitude about ever being able to meet a good man, one who would commit to her only. She came to see me for a private session, hoping to clear the way and save her heart from defeat. The door to relationship seemed to be closed. Several issues were in the way. One was the bad karma accumulated from dating the married man and her prolonged attachment to him. She needed to forgive herself for staying too long in a relationship that devalued her and had to let go of her continued desire for his love and respect. The second issue was her loyalty to an unmarried younger sister, whom she considered her best friend and believed was more worthy and deserving of happiness. She discovered that she had made an unconscious agreement not to marry before her sister. And third were her general feelings of unworthiness, caused by maternal neglect during early childhood. She had to confront all three and cleanse herself of the pain and karma. As she forgave herself within a guided visualization, she saw herself moving closer and closer to a door within her Stellar Heart. Once through the door's entrance, she was flooded with the light and harmony of the stellar union between her and her stellar twin. The experience brought her to tears and to the realization that there were no more obstacles to their reunion. We were both confident that she would meet her life partner soon.

Another woman with whom I had done a similar process and ceremony met her "match made in heaven" within months. In the ceremony, she forgave and cleared the obstacles to relationship and prayed to God that she would find her beloved. I ran into her in a supermarket four years later. She told me that she had met a man two months after the ceremony. They have been happily married now for over three years.

When there are obstacles to love, each one may need to be addressed and cleared in order to open the doors for complementary relationship. Obstacles can include deadly belief systems, such as negative attitudes about relationship, stereotypical attitudes about men or women, or fears about commitment in general. Some men, for example, fear commitment because they perceive it as entrapment. They are afraid that all their freedoms will be lost as soon as they turn outward from the altar and begin married life. They may desperately try to hold on to their youth, thinking that settling down may mean settling for less and losing the adventure.

Lack of self-esteem can close the door to the beloved. Women who view themselves as unattractive often shut the door of their hearts, unable to hear the call of their beloved. They may instead sit and yearn for a romantic ideal, a Prince Charming who will gallop up to their house and sweep them off their feet. Women like this perceive themselves as lost and imagine that to feel beautiful again, they must be discovered. However, their femininity may need to be coaxed out of the shadows of neglect before they will feel confident enough to venture out the door into the creative fields of their destinies.

Closely bonded relationships can clog the wheels of divine timing, disrupting the synergy between complements. A commitment to another marriage that is long over, clung to out of insecurity, will postpone our soul-mate reunion. These karmic relationships may have been necessary to prepare for the Real Thing, but they need to be dissolved once all the lessons of the relationship are over. They were presented on the stage of life to perform for a time, but their ghosts will linger if we don't clear the emotional bonds. The failure to forgive and end the emotional attachment to a previous relationship can create psychic interference that bars entrance to the new relationship. The clock of divine time may run into overtime if we hesitate too long.

Loyalties to our mother, father, sister or brother may also rob us of fulfillment. I remember a dream that I had shortly before my Divine Complement entered the picture. In the dream, there was a knock on the door, and when I opened it, he was standing there looking frustrated. I presented him with an owl wing as a gift. He said, "Come on. You are late." The dream baffled me because it was he who had prolonged the timing of our real meeting. However, my perception was limited by my logic. In examining the dream, I knew that the gift of the owl wing was my power and wisdom, which I was now ready to share with him. But why was I late? I went into my heart to investigate and saw that my mother possessed my heart. A symbiotic relationship with my mother had blocked the synergy and harmony between my complement and me enough to keep us apart. Even though my mother lived thousands of miles away, she could influence my dating choices as if I was a teenager living at home. Neither I nor my mother had any conscious desire to interfere in each other's lives, but our souls were enmeshed in the bonds of loyalty, love and unconscious needs. I must have had some help from angels from other dimensions, because the field of divine complementary harmony won the battle to bring my complement and me together at last.

Psychic connections with our parents are the most common bond that interferes with our soul's progress. Like vampires in the night, the psychic fangs of a mother or father may devour our opportunities. Unknown to us, they sneak into our heart and steal the life force with which, as the term implies, we create our life. They not only sap our strength but may infuse us with their negative beliefs and patterns, over-riding our own authentic intelligence. Their disharmony will interfere with our energy so much that our Divine Complement may not recognize us at all and will instead perceive the harmony of the symbiotic parent.

I see many people in my practice who live the unconscious lives of their parents or other close family members, rather than their authentic destinies. A young woman I counseled actually reproduced her grandmother's life, choosing a man who was 20 years her senior just as her grandmother had. When her complement arrived in her life, she was still married to this man. Her loyalty to the commitment was unreasonable because it depressed and degraded her, yet she was too insecure to end the relationship. She was in the shadow of her grandmother's philosophy: Marriage vows are forever even if you married the wrong person. This pattern postponed her marriage with her beloved by seven years while she fought with the shadow of her grandmother within her subconscious and developed the courage to leave. Some whose cultural or religious beliefs deny them the freedom to end a marriage in order to begin another may have a great deal of emotional conflict and guilt to contend with when presented the opportunity to embrace the beloved. They may believe it to be a transgression or a sin to leave their marriage even when their soul and spirit are shining the light elsewhere. The stellar promise, the most sacred promise, is our ultimate destination and takes precedence over other loyalties and commitments. To deny it is a severe transgression against our soul.

A woman I know in her late fifties was searching for her soul mate. However, searching in the darkness of someone else's energy and karma could no more produce relationship than could sitting at home knitting in front of the TV every

night. In the psychic dimension, she was symbiotically bonded to an older brother. The demands of this psychic connection were mainly her creation because she was trying to heal him out of a deep appreciation for the love he had offered her in many lifetimes. It was an unconscious desire that she could not have seen without the help of a clairvoyant. When I pointed it out to her, she said it all made perfect sense.

To clear the way of the disharmony of deadly psychic connections, we must first become aware that they exist. Illuminating them may be difficult without the spyglass of a third eye scanning our energy field and investigating our heart. Once revealed, it takes only prayers of forgiveness and the help of our angels to remove these connections from our psychic field. The process may need to be repeated again and again because psychic cords repeatedly reattach when one party desires affection so much that he or she repeatedly wanders into our field to make contact.

Divine Principle:
God does not create divine timing but can lovingly push it along at our request.

For some, life seems to have a perfect order, timing and result, even when it appears to others that fate has cast a cruel lot. Believing that the world is perfect in the end because God wants it this way or that the universe is always in perfect order is a common fatalistic and illusionary philosophy that denies the acknowledgement of free will, personal creative power and the integrity of the soul's choices. When the failure of a relationship or the death of a partner is explained as God's doing, it may unburden the heart, but such thinking may cast a shadow on our relationship with God. God's power never usurps our life or our creative design for fulfillment. However, God lovingly supports our strides in becoming divinely human, appreciating the growth steps we make by giving us gifts of grace.

Our reunion with our Divine Complement was always meant to be, but the missed opportunities and failures were *not* meant to be. Our divine plan is timed to push us through the door to do what we are meant to do to fulfill our karmic promises. We meet with our Divine Complement in the dimensions of the divine and synchronize our cosmic watches to the opening of our first act. We may have to re-synchronize them several times to make the curtain rise if we are lagging in our personal growth. At last, when the synergy is perfect, our complement may show up at the movie theater one night unaware that divine timing has scheduled the earthly reunion. It may have been synchronized only an hour before as our higher selves collaborated in the field of creativity. We may stand behind them at the concession stand, follow them down the aisle, and sit next to them as the curtain rises, unaware that it is the beginning of our own movie.

Serendipity may bring two together, but the conscious choices and efforts we make from that moment on will tie the knot. It is always our choice whether to give our all to the relationship and turn it into a lasting commitment or to deny the authentic identity of our complement and move on. If our choice is to move on, we may have some growing up to do in order to value the destiny and the person we were offered.

A second chance at a lasting relationship with our Divine Complement may be offered through conscious reconciliation or through a divine push. I ran into a couple at Starbucks who had been married for three years. The man told me it was their second time around. He said he had made some "very" serious mistakes almost 20 years ago when he and his complement first came together. He said he was not emotionally mature enough to commit and regretted it. It cost him 13 years of life with his beloved.

We may come full circle for another round of divine partnership if we have achieved emotional maturity. The obstacles to lasting relationship are often supreme lessons that illuminate the need for inner work. A long separation from our Divine Complement may protect them and us from the harsh consequences of behaviors that degrade and betray the integrity of our souls. If there are delays, postponements or even cancellation of a second chance, there is usually a good reason for it. Most likely, it is because there has not been enough spiritual and emotional growth to earn a second chance.

Divine Principle:
The memories of the heart grow fonder.

Our spiritual guidance and intuition may remind us that our soul mate is someone from our past. Perhaps there is a certain someone we have been unable to shake from our minds. We may dream of them frequently or hear the song we cherished as "our song" one too many times on the radio. We must not ignore signs or heart pangs and simply wait for some miracle to bring them back into our arms. We may have to write that important letter or make that phone call when our heart signals that it's time. We may very well have to track them down or pray for God's help in finding them.

Many complements do meet early on, but perhaps because they feel too young for marriage or their parents oppose the relationship, they drift apart. Later in life, dreams of their beloved may creep into the night as a reminder of the permanence of the divine connection. Sometimes these dreams will persist, demanding that action be taken in order to fulfill the destiny. Waiting, wishing and hoping will not fulfill the promise of relationship, especially if it's in the cards that one must seek out the other as a spiritual quest. It could even prove to be a long, heroic journey, something of the magnitude of searching for the Holy Grail.

I saw a segment on the TV show *It's a Miracle* about man in his fifties who had followed the thread of his yearnings to locate his long-lost sweetheart from high school. His life had had a long second act, during which he raised children with another woman, and he now found himself alone after his wife's death. He said that no matter where he was in his life, he couldn't forget his high school sweetheart and the passion he felt for her. It took him several years to find her, but when he did, he was not disappointed. She was as beautiful as he had remembered her. They both experienced the same sparks they felt for each other over 30 years before.

Another second-chance vignette came through my door with a friend who shared the story of her aunt who married her soul mate at the ripe age of 73. She and her beloved met in college, fell in love and wanted to get married right away. But the woman's parents objected so strongly that she felt it necessary to follow their commandment: "Thou shalt not waste your college education." She and her beloved soon parted, giving way to her parents' authorship of her life. Later, they married others, had children and lived what appeared to be fulfilling lives, but in truth at least one of them had not let go of the love for his twin. After his wife died—and more than 50 years after their broken engagement—he showed up on her doorstep and announced he still loved her. They were married that year.

Of course, not all first loves or high school and college sweethearts are the Real Thing, despite cherished memories of romantic love that we continue to long for. Once in a while, we hear a story of two who were steadies in high school and re-connect later in life to discover that they are soul mates. This story comes from a participant in an About.com survey on soul mates:

> *"Recently reunited with a high school steady—30-year reunion—sparks and flame—too much in common—way too much—and it has been a struggle to keep our minds rational—feelings and thoughts in unison—from great distances. Not experienced this type of aspect in any other relationship. ..."*

Stories like these may sound like second-chance miracles, "meant to be," or evidence of God's compassionate arm, but they more truly represent soul—and spirit-driven forces coupled with conscious collaboration to fulfill the stellar promise. So deeply is the stellar promise imprinted in Divine Complements' hearts that a full-circle return and second opportunity are likely after a first chance fell short. Such an opportunity comes better late than never.

Divine Principle:
Life may offer Divine Complements a second chance at love because their souls' deepest yearning is to be together.

The failure to recognize our Divine Complement as our perfect match and best choice can detour our life path off the Stellar Twin Highway. We may be separated for a long time until we earn a second chance.

I have a close friend whose second-chance story is an example of how the tides turn Divine Complements back to the origins of their love after they have been adrift for too long. She and her beloved met in college as freshmen and fell in love. They both recognized the deep soul connection that they shared and made plans to marry the next year. They were perfectly matched, with interests she described as wild and reckless. There was a strong psychic bond and sexual attraction that reinforced the commitment they made. They were certain they were making the right choice. The young man decided to take the summer to enjoy a surfing adventure in Mexico and vowed to return to his beloved with stories to tell. Young as she was and undoubtedly upset that he had abandoned her for so long, she began dating another man and decided to marry him instead. In her mind, he was a more logical and rational choice, as he was completing his law degree and appeared to have a foothold on the practical side of life.

She and her husband had two beautiful children, and for 20 years their relationship could have been described as solid and compatible, with a meaningful commitment to the family they created. However, in the last years she became more and more restless and disenchanted with her marriage. The cycle of karma with her husband was complete, and they agreed that the marriage was over. To others she may have appeared to be dismantling her life or in the midst of a midlife crisis, because she decided to let go of her career as a school vice principal at the same time. She said she was letting go of her false self, turning toward her spiritual self to create the life she deeply desired. She assumed it would be a life of her own making. On the *very day* she was moving out of the home she'd shared with her husband, she received a phone call that pointed her to the path that she had abandoned 20 years before. The call was from her Divine Complement, whom she had lost touch with after college. He asked her how she was and where she was in her life. At that moment, she realized that the creative promise between soul mates was greeting her a second time and that the path she thought she was forging for herself was being usurped for a divine purpose. She said she was taken aback and she thought to herself, "How did you know I just separated from my husband?" The answer, of course, was obvious. He had intuited an opening and the opportunity to be with the one he called "the love of his life," someone he had desired for 20 years.

In the psychic field and the spiritual dimensions, these complements remained in communion, always parallel on their individual paths. When she released the bonds of her commitment to her husband, her beloved's heart felt the light of an open field. He moved with his intuition to re-connect and begin fulfilling his part of their co-creative plan for a second chance.

Over the next month, they communicated regularly on the phone, catching up on the events of each other's lives. During their third conversation, he asked whether she had read anything interesting lately. She told him that she was reading an obscure book of Tibetan poetry, and to her great surprise, he told her that he was reading the same book and began to quote the poem she had just finished reading a moment earlier. As they communicated further in the coming weeks, they discovered many more synchronicities and commonalties in their interests and the paths they had chosen in their efforts to know God. All were evidence of the co-creative synergy that keeps two who were meant to be together in a harmony of equality and evolving at the same pace. She told me that when she received the first call from him, she knew in her heart that God was pushing them to their greater promise and purpose. She was certain that theirs would be a lasting and fulfilling relationship now that they had grown to emotional and spiritual maturity. She told me that it took her beloved a little longer to be sure, however. He was still married, and he had to make a transition that's extremely difficult for a man who's extremely loyal.

Two months later, they agreed it was time to meet face to face. She said that when he walked through the gate at the airport and she saw him, everything became crystal-clear in both their hearts. They were home.

Their path together over the past 10 years of their marriage has been an exciting spiritual journey marked by commitment to fulfill their promise to each other as Divine Complements. They walk the Red Road of Native American spirituality, helping each other to achieve more and more spiritual understanding and commitment to God. They are healers to each other, shedding light on the darker sides of their personalities, practicing conscious communication, and resolving any of their difficulties compassionately and respectfully. They serve their community by leading traditional sweat lodges and serving as spiritual elders, teaching those around them.

In sync, twin souls co-create a field of love at invisible dimensions, a field that produces parallel experiences and rewards their individual accomplishments. No matter how far apart they are in geography, their unified consciousness allows for distance learning so that they may remain on parallel paths in their evolution. It is one of most remarkable phenomena that twin souls can experience. Divine Complements can be on different continents, with a great divide between their souls, and still grow together after completing their individual and mutual lessons. As milestones are reached, they grow closer and closer until their paths merge again for a second chance.

Author's Endnote

By now, some of you may be wondering or questioning whether you are beside your authentic Divine Complement or have instead found your heart's desire with someone else. And many of you are still waiting and longing or looking around the corner to see whom you might have passed by or missed.

For those whose Divine Complements are anything but perfect, remember that human understanding is the key and consider that if you have loved and honored them enough and they have still fallen far short of their promises, perhaps it's time to let them go.

For those who want concrete proof of the Stellar Promise and of a divine destiny meant for two, they should look to the picture on the cover. What's always true is that inside our hearts lies the answer, the perfect match bonded and connected through a template of love hidden in the bridal chamber of the Stellar Heart. Should you reject the premise of this book—that there is only one person in the world and in all dimensions who matches you like a twin and with whom you will be forever bound through the Stellar Promise—you will discover its truth someday. Until then, suit your fancy, but ponder life's journey as a meaningful play.

And finally, for those who want more on the subject, this book's follow-up, *Divine Complement Forever*, offers more on the legacy of Jesus and Mary Magdalene, heartfelt stories and further exploration of the mysterious dimensions of twin-soul communion, the bonds of commitment, destiny's children, same-sex complements, and the experiences of complements separated by divorce or death.

Glossary of Terms

Anima—The feminine aspect of the soul. It is the receptive principle and intuitive emotional intelligence.

Animus—The masculine aspect of the soul. It is the active principle and rational intelligence.

Bridal Chamber—The innermost chamber of the Stellar Heart matrix containing the harmonic code signature of twin souls. Initiations of the bridal chamber offer us direct experiences of communion with our twin soul and with God.

Destiny—One's potentials and higher purpose for an individual lifetime. The soul carries the blueprint for its destiny along with its personality potentials and talents for the incarnation.

Divine Complement—Our twin soul and twin flame. They represent that one person to whom we are most connected soul-to-soul and spirit-to-spirit, and with whom we may be offered the

247

opportunity to meet and bond with at the human dimension. They hold inborn potentials that match and complement our own and hold the key to our spiritual evolution. They are our ultimate complementary partner.

Divine Consciousness—A state of awareness, much like enlightenment, when one recognizes the more meaningful dimensions of existence, such as our soul-to-soul connections, karmic responsibilities and our higher purpose.

Fate—A universal law and cosmic principle that offers us our just due, what we deserve as opposed to what we think we deserve. The Greeks have a beautiful name for fate, Moira, the cosmic principle of binding apportionment. Moira selects and distributes our "due portion" in life, whether it is in the form of financial opportunities or opportunities for loving friendships.

Hieros gamos—An ancient sacred sexual ritual usually between a King and a hierodule (sacred prostitute), two sacred lovers, consummating love in spiritual communion to touch the divine within themselves. In Mesopotamia, the *hieros gamos* ritual was thought to ensure the well-being of the king, the prosperity of the people and the continued fertility of the land.

Higher Purpose—A fulfilling path such as a career choice of service or a commitment to serve one's children or partner. When fulfilled, our higher purpose will redeem our soul.

Inner Marriage—The integrated balance of the masculine and feminine aspects, intuitive and rational intelligence, applied towards the fulfillment of our higher purpose or destiny.

Karma—The weight of cause and effect on the soul and life of the individual. Most commonly used to define the weight of transgressions on the individual, as in the 'debt of the soul'.

Love's Intelligence—The idea that love is intelligent and compassionate, transcending our lower emotional needs and ordinary responses. When we consciously apply its principles, it positively transforms our relationships and interactions.

Oversoul—Our Spirit, angelic-self, or higher-self residing at the 6th dimension. The oversoul is unified with God and exhibits our highest creative potentials.

Sacred Union—Refers to the spiritual bonds between Divine Complements or Twin Souls as representing a sacred covenant.

Serendipity—A magical and meaningful meeting of happenstance.

Soul—The multi-dimensional evolutionary body termed "The Self" by Jungian psychology. The soul contains evolutionary memory of the collective legacy of human experience, memories of its previous incarnations, archetypal imprints, and the Anima/Animus (male and female aspects). It is defined through its accumulative evolutionary experiences.

Soul Mate—A unique and complementary partner who is intimately bonded to us at the soul level. A term sometimes used synonymously with Twin Soul and Divine Complement, but more often viewed as one of many possible matches.

Spirit—Also known as the Oversoul, Stellar Body, Angelic Self and Higher self. It is defined as the divine body or spiritual essence of each individual. It transcends the physical and is in constant connection and communion with God.

Stellar Heart—The crystalline chamber and structure of the heart chakra, an energy center that contains the heart matrix of the oversoul.

Stellar Matrix—An intricate mosaic of unique attributes and radiant colored harmonies that forms the essence of one's spirit or divine body. It is a part of the Stellar Heart and resides at the sixth dimension.

Stellar Promise—The eternal commitment between twin souls.

Synchronicity—Repetitive meaningful signs that emerge out of a creative field of consciousness, usually leading towards personal fulfillment. It represents a meaningful coincidence or magical occurrence with symbolic value.

Template of Love—Synonymous with the Heart Matrix or Stellar Matrix.

Twin Soul or Twin Flame—Our perfect complementary match—our Divine Complement. They are the one person who is linked to us through the bridal chamber of the Stellar Heart in an eternal commitment spirit-to-spirit and soul-to-soul. As a twin reflection of complementary qualities, they are in our life to serve as a mirror of the masculine or feminine within us and often reflect our least integrated qualities, talents and potentials.

References

Ball, Lucille. *Love Lucy*. New York: Berkeley Boulevard Books, a division of Penguin Putman Inc., 1996

Burns, George. *Gracie: A Love Story*. New York: G. P. Putman's Sons, 1988.

Gardner, Laurence. *Bloodline of The Holy Grail*. Massachusetts: Element Book Limited, 1996.

Graves, Robert. *The Green Myths: Combined Edition*. New York: Penguin Books, 1992

Lincoln, Henry. *Holy Blood, Holy Grail*. New York: Dell Publishing Group Inc., 1982

Robinson, James M. *The Nag Hammadi Library*. New York: Harper San Francisco, 1990.

Starbird, Margaret. *The Woman with the Alabaster Jar: Mary Magdalene and the Holy Grail*. Vermont: Bear & Company, 1993.

Starbird, Margaret. The Goddess in the Gospels: Reclaiming the Sacred Feminine. Vermont: Bear & Company, 1998

Starbird, Margaret. *Magdalene's Lost Legacy: Symbolic Numbers and The Sacred Union in Christianity.* Vermont: Bear & Compnay, 2003.

The Holy Bible: King James Version.

Williamson, Marianne. *Enchanted Love: The Mystical Power of Intimate Relationships.* New York: Simon & Schuster, 1999.

Woodman, Marion. *The Ravaged Bridegroom.* Toronto, Canada: Inner City Books,1990.

Index

Author's Offers and Contact

Ariadne Green is a dream expert and spiritual teacher who facilitates workshops and trainings in the Art of Shamanism and dream work internationally. She makes her home on the Hawaiian island of Maui. A complete schedule of speaking engagements, workshops and events as well as information on how to sponsor an event in your area is listed on her website: www. ariadnegreen.com.

Magdalene's Rose, the twin centered rose and divine emanation used on the cover of this book, is available as a set of beautiful all occasion greeting cards designed by Carol Quan, photo collage artist. Ordering information can be obtained on Ariadne's website.

Contact the author through her website at:

www.ariadnegreen.com